Knowledge Resources for the Socio-Economic Sciences and Humanities 2017

AA001503

Varna, Bulgaria
7 September 2017

Editors:

Kalliopi Zervanou
Petya Osenova
Eveline Wandl-Vogt
Dan Cristea

ISBN: 978-1-5108-5548-9

Printed from e-media with permission by:

Curran Associates, Inc.
57 Morehouse Lane
Red Hook, NY 12571

Some format issues inherent in the e-media version may also appear in this print version.

Copyright© (2017) by the Association for Computational Linguistics
All rights reserved.

Printed by Curran Associates, Inc. (2018)

For permission requests, please contact the Association for Computational Linguistics at the address below.

Association for Computational Linguistics
209 N. Eighth Street
Stroudsburg, Pennsylvania 18360

Phone: 1-570-476-8006
Fax: 1-570-476-0860

acl@aclweb.org

Additional copies of this publication are available from:

Curran Associates, Inc.
57 Morehouse Lane
Red Hook, NY 12571 USA
Phone: 845-758-0400
Fax: 845-758-2633
Email: curran@proceedings.com
Web: www.proceedings.com

Knowledge Resources for the Socio-Economic

Sciences and Humanities

PROCEEDINGS

Edited by
Kalliopi Zervanou, Petya Osenova, Eveline Wandl-Vogt, Dan Cristea

Varna, Bulgaria

7 September, 2017

Knowledge Resources for the Socio-Economic
Sciences and Humanities

PROCEEDINGS

Varna, Bulgaria
7 September 2017

Designed and Printed by INCOMA Ltd.
Shoumen, BULGARIA

Preface

Big cultural heritage data present an unprecedented opportunity for the humanities that is reshaping conventional research methods. However, digital humanities have grown past the stage where the mere availability of digital data was enough as a demonstrator of possibilities. Knowledge resource modeling, development, enrichment and integration is crucial for associating relevant information in pools of digital material which are not only scattered across various archives, libraries and collections, but they also often lack relevant metadata. Within this research framework, NLP approaches originally stemming from lexico-semantic information extraction and knowledge resource representation, modeling, development and reuse have a pivotal role to play.

From the NLP perspective, applications of knowledge resources for the Socio-Economic Sciences and Humanities present numerous interesting research challenges that relate among others to the development of historical lexico-semantic sources and annotated corpora, addressing ambiguity and variation in historical sources and the development of knowledge resources for NLP tool adaptation purposes, using NLP techniques for semantic interlinking, mapping, and integration of existing knowledge resources. Moreover, a recently renewed interest in linguistic linked data approaches to language resources presents both a challenge and an opportunity for NLP researchers working in the Socio-Economic Sciences and Humanities domains, for linking cultural heritage and humanities data sources to linguistic linked data information.

The papers in this proceedings cover various topics, such as: methods to linking heterogeneous datasets in Humanities; construction of resources that contain old data or serve for the purposes of eLearning in the area of foreign language teaching; a general framework for modeling perspectives, for example in biographies; machine learning techniques for the purposes of linguistic typology and diachronic language comparison.

The Organizers

The KnowRSH workshop is organised by:

Kalliopi Zervanou (Co-chair), Utrecht University, The Netherlands

Petya Osenova (Co-chair), Bulgarian Academy of Sciences, Bulgaria

Eveline Wandl-Vogt, Austrian Academy of Sciences, Austria

Dan Cristea, "Alexandru Ioan Cuza" University of Iasi, Romania

The KnowRSH workshop is endorsed by:

the ACL Special Interest Group on Language Technologies
for the Socio-Economic Sciences and Humanities (SIGHUM)

DARIAH-EU Working Group for Lexical Resources

COST ENeL

Program Committee:

Jeannine Beeken (UK Data Archive, University of Essex, UK)
Verginica Barbu Mititelu (RACAI Bucuresti, Romania)
António Branco (University of Lisbon, Portugal)
Paul Buitelaar (National University of Ireland, Galway, Ireland)
Nicoletta Calzolari (Institute for Computational Linguistics "A. Zampolli", National Research Council of Italy, Italy)
Christian Chiarcos (Goethe-Universität Frankfurt am Main, Germany)
Thierry Declerck (DFKI GmbH, Germany)
Maud Ehrmann (École Polytechnique Fédérale de Lausanne, Switzerland)
Antske Fokkens (Vrije Universiteit Amsterdam, The Netherlands)
Flavius Frasincar (Erasmus Universiteit Rotterdam, The Netherlands)
Daniela Gifu ("Alexandru Ioan Cuza" University of Iasi, Romania)
Sebastian Hellmann (AKSW University of Leipzig, Germany)
Jaap Kamps (Universiteit van Amsterdam, The Netherlands)
Hannah Kermes (Universität des Saarlandes, Germany)
Stasinos Konstantopoulos (National Centre of Scientific Research "Demokritos", Greece)

Marijn Koolen (Huygens ING (KNAW), The Netherlands)
John Philip McCrae (National University of Ireland, Galway, Ireland)
Nirmala Menon (Indian Institute of Technology Indore, India)
Albert Meroño Peñuela (Vrije Universiteit Amsterdam, The Netherlands)
Kristoffer Nielbo (Aarhus University, Denmark)
Constantin Orasan (University of Wolverhampton, UK)
Marco Passarotti (Universita Cattolica del Sacro Cuore, Italy)
Maciej Piasecki (Wroclaw University of Technology, Poland)
Davide Picca (Université de Lausanne, Switzerland)
Michael Piotrowski (Université de Lausanne, Switzerland)
Martin Reynaert (Tilburg University, Radboud University Nijmegen, The Netherlands)
Renato Rocha Souza (Fundação Getulio Vargas, Brazil)
Matteo Romanello (École Polytechnique Fédérale de Lausanne, Switzerland)
Liudmila Rychkova (Yanka Kupala State University of Grodno, Belarus)
Marijn Schraagen (Utrecht University, The Netherlands)
Claudia Soria (Institute for Computational Linguistics "A. Zampolli",
National Research Council of Italy, Italy)
Caroline Sporleder (Georg-August-Universität Göttingen, Germany)
Carlo Strapparava (Fondazione Bruno Kessler, Italia)
Cristina Vertan (University of Hamburg, Germany)
Michael Zock (CNRS-LIF, France)

Table of Contents

Connecting people digitally - a semantic web based approach to linking heterogeneous data sets

Katalin Lejtovicz, Amelie Dorn
Austrian Centre for Digital Humanities, Vienna, Austria
{katalin.lejtovicz, amelie.dorn}@oeaw.ac.at

Abstract

In this paper we present a semantic enrichment approach for linking two distinct data sets: the ÖBL (Austrian Biographical Dictionary) and the dbo@ema (Database of Bavarian Dialects in Austria electronically mapped). Although the data sets are different in their content and in the structuring of data, they contain similar common "entities" such as names of persons. Here we describe the semantic enrichment process of how these data sets can be inter-linked through URIs (Uniform Resource Identifiers) taking person names as a concrete example. Moreover, we also point to societal benefits of applying such semantic enrichment methods in order to open and connect our resources to various services.

1 Introduction

In the Digital Humanities discourse, the establishment of data networks and creation of links between different resources has been a key aspect. The linking of resources not only aims at enrichment, but more importantly also at providing wider access to data resources in local but also global digital infrastructures. As a consequence data use and re-use is enabled.

One widely practised way of enabling semantic enrichment and linking is by means of open-source tools relying on semantic web technologies. For example DBpedia Spotlight (Mendes et al., 2011) provides the possibility to automatically annotate documents with mentions of DBpedia resources. The tool uses as resource types the classes of the DBpedia Ontology, thus enabling the user to annotate documents with 272 different entity types. Furthermore, the user can choose the annotation domain by selecting the classes of the Ontology or by defining them via a SPARQL query. Although DBpedia Spotlight is a powerful tool, it limits entity linking to only one resource, and was developed for the English language. To apply it on documents written in other languages, the models used by Spotlight have to be adapted. Babelfy (Moro et al., 2014) uses a graph-based approach to perform entity linking and word sense disambiguation, relying on BabelNet 1.1.1 - a semantic network of Wikipedia and WordNet[1] - in order to provide LOD[2] links to identified text fragments. Babelfy's main asset is the use of a multilingual resource that incorporates encyclopedic knowledge as well, however it has the drawback, that the resources used for word sense disambiguation and entity linking cannot be defined or chosen by the user. For knowledge networks to be created across resources and applied to various data sets, there is a need for data to be processed by means of computational linguistic tools and matched preferably against domain specific authority resources.

In this paper we introduce and exemplify such a linking process developed and applied in the context of two connected Digital Humanities projects, APIS[3] (Lejtovicz et al., 2015) and exploreAT![4] (Wandl-Vogt et al, 2015; Benito et al., 2016; Dorn et al, 2016). The diverse digital networks available to-date have been created around a variety of topics. Some

[1] https://wordnet.princeton.edu/ [last accessed: 23.06.2017]
[2] http://lod-cloud.net/ [last accessed: 23.06.2017]
[3] https://www.oeaw.ac.at/acdh/projects/apis/ [last accessed: 23.06.2017]
[4] https://www.oeaw.ac.at/acdh/projects/exploreat/ [last accessed: 23.06.2017]

Proceedings of Knowledge Resources for the Socio-Economic Sciences and Humanities associated with RANLP-17, pages 1–8, Varna, Bulgaria, 7 Sep 2017.

evolve around networks of places (The Historical GIS Research Network[5]) or of art (e.g. EuropeanaArt[6]), etc. In our case, we apply semantic web tools to interlink person names. In the Digital Humanities project APIS, it is a main goal to unveil connections among people in biographical sources, which provides insightful information on the lives of well-known people. Applying entity-linking in connection with relation extraction - a task addressed in the project APIS - allows us to identify and visualize connections among entities mentioned in different data sources.

This study thus aims at linking existing resources partly containing the same information through the use of semantic web technologies. Through the additional enrichment with LOD, our study aims to show how these data sets can first be connected, and later opened to a wider user audience. This in turn adds to their prolonged re-use and sustainability by ensuring that additions and corrections to the data set only have to be added once to the reference resource, instead of updating all the distinct data resources. In addition, the results of our study also contribute to making information on people networks more widely available also to knowledge society.

2 Data and resources

The data behind the inter-linking process of the projects APIS and exploreAT! are extracted from the resources ÖBL (Austrian Biographical Dictionary; Gruber and Feigl, 2009) and dbo@ema[7] (Database of Bavarian Dialects in Austria electronically mapped) (cf. Wandl-Vogt et al., 2008). In the realization of both projects, the Austrian Centre for Digital Humanities (ACDH-ÖAW[8]) plays an important role. They rely on data from the respective resources (ÖBL, dbo@ema) which contain similar types of elements such as persons, locations, institutions and titles of written works. In ÖBL this concerns the names of important historical figures, names of cities and countries relevant to the lives of the people in the biographies, as well as titles of books, journals, or publications mentioned in the biographies. In the dbo@ema, on the other hand, we are dealing with names of locations and regions, names of data collectors or authors and also titles of dictionaries, dissertations and literature. The benefit of linking the above mentioned data sets resides in the possibility to enrich the biographies with missing information contained in the entries of the dbo@ema and vice versa. Often for example the list of literature works is incomplete in either ÖBL or dbo@ema, by linking the two resources, the missing information can be added the other resource.

The ***ÖBL*** contains around 18.500 biographies and serves as the reference work for APIS, a project which aims to investigate whether a large scale lexicon can be used as the basis of quantitative data analysis and how biographical research can benefit from the digital transformation process realized in APIS. The lexicon contains biographies of important historical figures from the Austro-Hungarian Monarchy having lived in the time period of 1815-1950. The data is not only published in print, but it is also available in the machine readable XML format for the APIS project. An example of a typical ÖBL data entry in XML format is provided in Appendix. It is taken from the biography of *Johann Willibald Nagl*, an Austrian writer and germanist having lived and worked on the turn of the century. The entry contains some structured information in XML elements such as *Geburt* (containing place and date of birth), however the majority of the information (in this specific example referring to the studies and the career path of August Schreiber) is embedded in the unstructured XML element *Haupttext* (i.e. main text). The ÖBL data set contains not only the 18.500 persons the biographies were written about but also additional individuals mentioned in the main text. This set of names together with the persons in dbo@ema creates the basis for connecting the two projects APIS and exploreAT! via an automatic alignment process.

The dbo@ema, on the other hand is to-date a part of the Database of Bavarian dialects in Austria (DBÖ) which forms the basis of the project exploreAT!. The project explores this

[5] http://www.hgis.org.uk/ [accessed: 23.06.2017]

[6] http://www.europeana.eu/portal/de/collections/art [accessed: 23.06.2017]

[7] https://wboe.oeaw.ac.at/projekt/beschreibung/ [accessed: 23.06.2017]

[8] https://www.oeaw.ac.at/acdh/acdh-home/ [accessed: 23.06.2017]

large heterogeneous collection of 20th century dialect data of the Bavarian dialects in Austria from perspectives of cultural lexicography, semantic technologies, visual analysis and citizen science. The dbo@ema is a MySQL database that comprises of a collection of dialect words of various fields of everyday life. Part of the database comprises of the digitised data originally collected by means of paper questionnaires as well as the digitized entries of the plants (~32.000 headwords) and mushrooms collections (~ 1.000 headwords), also include names of places and regions in the former Austro-Hungarian Empire, as well as names of data collectors or authors of dictionaries, dissertations or literature. Data concerning persons involved in the collection are for the bigger part derived from internal archival material of the institute. Initially, the available questionnaire data was manually entered in TUSTEP (TUebingen System of TExt processing Programs)[9], a professional toolbox for scholarly processing of textual data. All in all, the DBÖ counts around 3.5 million records and an estimated 200,000 headwords.

3 Applying semantic web technologies to inter-link heterogeneous DH data sets

In many projects dealing with digital collections, digital content is generated from scanned books, dictionaries, maps, etc. This is, however, just the prerequisite for establishing a knowledge base which is usable and reusable within and across different disciplines. In order to make data more widely available in a network of relevant sources, the enrichment with Linked Open Data (LOD) is key. Enrichment is a process that has to be established in order to open up DH data sets (e.g. lexicons, encyclopedia, dictionaries, etc.) not only to the public, but also to the members of the research community and to industry.

The projects APIS and exploreAT! face the challenge that the valuable information they contain is embedded in different data models and data formats, and therefore they are not completely transparent and reusable for the researchers, domain experts and interested citizens. It is also the case in many other Digital Humanities (DH) projects that they partially comprise of the same information embedded in different resources. APIS and exploreAT! have common entity types, among them being persons, locations, names of written works, which when being identified and aligned, can serve as the basis for inter-linking the two projects. This allows for adding missing information from the complementary data set, uncovering and visualizing networks of common entities, and expanding the search space by introducing new, joined data sets to the previously limited research environment.

The motivation to semantically enrich the ÖBL data collection - a historically and culturally rich heritage data - is a main goal in the APIS project. We designed a workflow that is also applicable for the semantic annotation of other DH collections as well. This workflow is set up by first identifying candidates for the linking process, in the second step linking them automatically to LOD resources and finally approving and curating the results. In our study, we link entities to GeoNames and GND, and plan to further extend the pool of used LOD resources with VIAF[10]. We use the linked LOD resources to enrich our data with missing information (e.g. to add name variants, latitude, longitude, if available URI of corresponding Wikipedia article, etc. to our data sets), to detect possible errors in our data sets by comparing the information in ÖBL/dbo@ema with the information contained in GeoNames/GND, and to make it machine readable and searchable through publishing it eventually in the LOD cloud. However linking to significant vocabularies such as GeoNames and GND do not only provide valuable information, but also challenge computational linguistic systems. Some of the problems are caused by the incompleteness of authority files, not all person/place/institution names are contained in LOD vocabularies. However this problem can be addressed by adding further resources to the system, for this reason we are planning to index VIAF in addition to GeoNames and GND. If an entity is present in a vocabulary, information in

[9] www.tustep.uni-tuebingen.de/ [last accessed: 23.06.2017]

[10] https://viaf.org/ [last accessed: 23.06.2017]

a biography might still not be enough to automatically identify the connection. Often the only information about spouses, siblings, tutors, etc. mentioned in the biography are their name and their relationship (father of, spouse, tutor of, etc.) to the person the biography was written about. In this case relation extraction can help to correctly identifying the matching entity. Relational information collected from the biographies can be compared with information in the dictionaries, and in case of matching values, the link between the entities can be proposed by the system. In APIS we implemented a rule based approach using the JAPE[11] grammar to detect relations. Further difficulties arise from names, where more than one match is possible with vocabulary entries. Choosing the correct match is called disambiguation, the heuristics we apply for automatic disambiguation consist of fine-tuning the Solr indexes of place names and person names, and adapting them to the characteristics of the input data. We apply heuristics such as indexing only person names from geographical areas relevant to the data sets ÖBL and dbo@ema. Thus we can decrease false matches caused by name-collisions between individuals having born, lived and died in areas other than ÖBL/ dbo@ema related ones.

For the realization of the entity linking, Apache Stanbol[12] has been chosen as an open-source, customizable and extendible implementation framework to work with. The benefit of using Apache Stanbol is, on the one hand its ability to create Referenced Sites (i.e. a local Apache Solr[13] index of a knowledge base) from any (publicly available) RDF-XML resource and to perform Entity Linking against the compiled site. Furthermore, Stanbol allows the user to take advantage of the integrated Natural Language Processing (NLP) frameworks such as OpenNLP[14] in a free, open source environment. In APIS we have set up a procedure to convert unstructured, full text biographies into structured, semantically enriched and machine-readable documents. This procedure currently consists of two steps. First, we resolve the abbreviations including the shortened forms of person names, institution names, academic titles, location names, frequent verbs, etc. with a regular expression based Java program to substitute them with their corresponding resolution taken from an ÖBL-intern abbreviations list. Second, we configure and run Stanbol's Entityhub Indexing Tool to create Solr indexes from the resources GeoNames[15] and GND[16] After initializing the index an Enhancement Chain is set up. The Enhancement Chain is on the one hand responsible for running NLP tasks on the biographies (language detection, sentence splitting, tokenization, part-of-speech tagging and chunking) and on the other hand for matching the entities identified by the NLP processor with the Solr index. In our project, the NLP pipeline runs the OpenNLP software with the German model files.

Although correction methods can reduce the error rate of automatic Entity Linking, some manual correction is still required, hence we foresee a manual data curation process to complement and correct the shortcomings of the automatic process.

4 Data set analysis

Analyzing the person names in the data sets ÖBL and dbo@ema the following figures emerged: in the ÖBL (counting the biographies written until the beginning of the project) life stories of 18219 persons comprise the data set of the APIS project, whereas the dbo@ema data resource contains 8841 person names. When aligning the two data sets, results showed that 402 person names are identical, given the criteria that the first name and the last name of the corresponding dbo@ema and ÖBL entries have to match exactly. Due to the fact, that the two data sets differ in how they model personal data (e.g. the ÖBL *second name* contains all the name variants of a person in a comma separated format, whereas the dbo@ema contains a comma in the *second name* before noble titles) the number of matches between the two

[11] https://gate.ac.uk/sale/tao/splitch8.html [last accessed: 23.06.2017]
[12] https://stanbol.apache.org/ [last accessed: 23.06.2017]
[13] http://lucene.apache.org/solr/ [last accessed: 23.06.2017]
[14] https://opennlp.apache.org/ [last accessed: 23.06.2017]

[15] http://www.geonames.org/about.html [last accessed: 23.06.2017]
[16] http://www.dnb.de/EN/Standardisierung/GND/gnd_node.html [last accessed: 23.06.2017]

resources could be higher after reconciliation. Our analysis thus shows a first rough estimation about how many persons are potentially overlapping in the two collections. Further manual curation is necessary considering that information for the correct identification of a person is often missing in the database. The dbo@ema often lacks the information about date and place of birth. In this case additional knowledge, such as the publications or names of relatives can be used to identify and correctly find the person from the dbo@ema in the Austrian Biographical Dictionary. When narrowing down the criteria to exactly match on the first name, last name and year of birth, there are only 35 entries found that occur in both resources. The small number of matches can also be attributed to the fact, that in many cases basic information is missing for the exact identification of a person. To overcome this problem, a system has been developed in the frame of the APIS project, where manual curation of entities such as persons, locations, institutions, works and events is possible. We foresee that a manual review process will be carried out after the automatic linking of the dbo@ema and ÖBL person data sets, in order to approve correctly established links, revise erroneous connections and add missing information to both data sources.

The following example illustrates how the knowledge sources ÖBL and dbo@ema are connected to each other via the GND URI assigned to *Johann Willibald Nagl*, an Austrian writer and Germanist appearing in both data sets. Nagls ÖBL biography has been published online, and his personal data (name, date and place of birth, date and place of death) is also recorded in the dbo@ema database (see the two entries of Nagl in the Appendix). The link between the two instances has been established by means of the Stanbol Entity Linking Module, which identifies *Johann Willibald Nagl* as a candidate for entity matching and looks it up in the Solr index created from GND person names. Below we show an excerpt of the semantic annotation created by Stanbol. The URI http://d-nb.info/gnd/116880414 links the two occurrences of *Johann Willibald Nagl* and thus the two resources ÖBL and dboe@ema.


```
{
  "@id": "urn:enhancement-41adec0e-9ebc-8d19-7644-b799288d563b",
  "@type": [
  "Enhancement",
  "EntityAnnotation"
  ],
  "confidence": 1.0,
  "created": "2017-06-22T16:25:27.384Z",
  "creator": "org.apache.stanbol.enhancer.engines.entitylinking.engine.EntityLinkingEngine",
  "entity-label": "Nagl, Johann Willibald",
  "entity-reference": "http://d-nb.info/gnd/116880414",
  "entity-type": "http://d-nb.info/standards/elementset/gnd#DifferentiatedPerson",
  "extracted-from": "urn:content-item-sha1-3dee9b203b74c12fec298348e74a1a0f16ee7da2",
  "relation": "urn:enhancement-e1a4dcdd-e9fc-d9fc-42d4-b4e7cabb4685",
  "site": "gndPersons"
  }
```


With the help of a web application being developed in APIS we are planning to evaluate the quality of the linking process. The application is designed to support automatic and manual annotation within one system, thus allowing automatic evaluation of annotation tasks.

5 Discussion and Conclusion

In this paper we discussed the linking of person names in two data sets, the ÖBL and dbo@ema. Our applied method has shown, that through the automatic entity linking process, the same persons occurring in different resources can be detected and connected. Through the established links and by applying the relation extraction method implemented in the APIS project, a link across the data sets ÖBL and dbo@ema can be revealed, giving valuable information of relations among persons mentioned. Our method is only in its developing stages and this paper is a first introduction. By generating person networks including additional information existent in the ÖBL or dbo@ema, our "social network" could provide a valuable source of information also for non-specialists. As persons mentioned in the two resources are also connected to a variety of personal information (profession, birth place, etc.), opening up and connecting our data sets to other services for societal benefits is another main goal. Services that could potentially benefit from our generated knowledge include Europeana collections or Museums. Connecting the information from our ÖBL and dbo@ema resources to current collections would offer a fruitful collaboration for giving citizens access to otherwise hidden information.

References

Benito, A., Losada, A. G., Therón, R., Dorn, A., Seltmann, M., Wandl-Vogt, E. (2016): A spatio-temporal visual analysis tool for historical dictionaries. TEEM 2016. Proceedings of the Fourth International Conference on Technological Ecosystems for Enhancing Multiculturality: pp. 985-990

Gruber, C., Feigl, R. (2009) Von der Karteikarte zum biografischen Informationsmanagementsystem. Neue Wege am Institut Österreichisches Biographisches Lexikon und biographische Dokumentation, in: Martina Schattkowsky / Frank Metasch (eds.), Biografische Lexika im Internet. Internationale Tagung der „Sächsischen Biografie" in Dresden (30. und 31. Mai 2008) (= Bausteine aus dem Institut für Sächsische Geschichte und Volkskunde 14), Dresden: Thelem Universitätsverlag, 2009, pp. 55–75

Dorn, A., Wandl-Vogt, E., Bowers, J., Piringer, B., Seltmann, M. (2016) exploreAT! – perspectives of exploring a dialect language resource in a framework of European digital infrastructures.1st Interna-tional Congress on Sociolinguistics (ICS-1), Budapest, Hungary.

Lejtovicz, K., Durco, M., Schlögl, M., Wandl-Vogt, E. (2015) APIS New Austrian Prosopographical Information System. Mapping Historical Networks. 2nd DHA Conference. Vienna, Austria. DOI: 10.15169/sci-gaia:1473321487.86

Mendes, Pablo N., Jakob, Max, García-Silva, Andrés, and Bizer, Christian, "DBpedia spotlight: shedding light on the web of documents". In: Proceedings of the 7th International Conference on Semantic Systems, page 1-8. New York, NY, USA, ACM, (2011)

Moro, A., Raganato, A., Navigli, R. (2014) Entity Linking meets Word Sense Disambiguation: a Unified Approach. Transactions of the Association for Computational Linguistics (TACL), 2, pp. 231-244.

Schopper, D., Bowers J., Wandl-Vogt, E (2015) dboe@TEI: remodelling a database of dialects into a rich LOD resource. Proceedings of TEI conference 2015.

Wandl-Vogt, E., Bartelme, N., Fliedl, G., Hassler, M., Kop, C., Mayr, H., Nickel, J., Scholz, J., Vöhringer, J. (2008): dbo@ema. A system for archiving, handling and mapping heterogeneous dialect data for dialect dictionaries. In: Bernal, Elisenda / De Cesaris, Janet (Hrsg.): Proceedings of the XIII Euralex International Congress, Barcelona, Universitat Pompeu Fabra, 15.-19. Juli 2008 (= Sèrie activitats 20). Barcelona (Documenta Universitaria). S. 1467-1472 (CD-ROM).

Wandl-Vogt, E., Kieslinger, B., O´Connor, A., Theron, R. (2015). „exploreAT! Perspektiven einer Transformation am Beispiel eines lexikographischen Jahrhundertprojekts", in: DHd-Tagung 2015. Graz. Austria. Accessed at: http://dhd2015.uni-graz.at [23.06.2017]

Appendix

ÖBL entry of Johann Willibald Nagl:


```
<?xml version="1.0" encoding="utf-8"?>
<Eintrag xmlns="http://www.biographien.ac.at"
xmlns:xsi="http://www.w3.org/2001/XMLSchema-instance"
xsi:schemaLocation="http://www.biographien.ac.at
https://aspix2.lgbs.at/GIDEON_NG_OEBL/userdefined/Biografien/XML/XSD/OEBL-Bio-V1.xsd"
Nummer="Nagl_Johann-Willibald_1856_1918.xml"
Version="01" pnd="116880414"
eoebl_id="1410752">
    <Lexikonartikel>
      <Schlagwort>
        <Hauptbezeichnung>Nagl</Hauptbezeichnung>
        <Nebenbezeichnung Type="Vorname">Johann Willibald</Nebenbezeichnung>
      </Schlagwort>
      <Sortierung_Nachname>Nagl</Sortierung_Nachname>
```

<Sortierung_Vorname>Johann Willibald</Sortierung_Vorname>

<Schlagwort_Nachname>Nagl</Schlagwort_Nachname>
<Schlagwort_Vorname>Johann Willibald</Schlagwort_Vorname>
<Vita>
<Geburt Metadatum="1856" TT="11" MM="5">(1856-<Geographischer_Begriff OrtAlt="Natschbach b. Neunkirchen" OrtNeu="?" LandAlt="NÖ" LandNeu="Österreich/NÖ">Natschbach b. Neunkirchen (?, NÖ)</Geographischer_Begriff></Geburt>
<Tod Metadatum="1918" TT="23" MM="7">1918)<Geographischer_Begriff OrtAlt="Diepolz b. Neunkirchen" OrtNeu="?" LandAlt="NÖ" LandNeu="Österreich/NÖ">Diepolz b. Neunkirchen (?, NÖ)</Geographischer_Begriff></Tod>
<Beruf Berufsgruppe="Geisteswissenschaft"> Germanist und Schriftsteller</Beruf>
<Beruf Berufsgruppe="Literatur, Buch- und Zeitungswesen" />
</Vita>
<Geschlecht Type="m" />
<Kurzdefinition>Nagl Johann Willibald, Germanist und Schriftsteller. * Natschbach b. Neunkirchen (NÖ), 11. 5. 1856; † Diepolz b. Neunkirchen (NÖ), 23. 7. 1918.</Kurzdefinition>
<Haupttext>Stud. nach einem bald wieder abgebrochenen Theol.-Stud. Phil. und Germanistik an der Univ. Wien, 1886 Dr. phil. Neben seiner Lehrtätigkeit an verschiedenen Schulen war N. ab 1890 als Priv. Doz. für Mundartforschung an der Univ. Wien tätig. Er darf neben Seemüller zu den Initiatoren der Wr. mundartkundlichen Schule (z. B. als Hrsg. der Z. „Deutsche Mundarten") gezählt werden, wenn auch manche von ihm angeschnittene Probleme später anderen Lösungen zugeführt wurden. Schon als Schottenkleriker hatte N. begonnen, die alte Tierfabel von Reineke Fuchs in seiner niederösterr. Heimatmundart darzustellen. Als Vorlage für das Dialektepos „Der Fuchs Roáner, á lehrreichs und kürzweiligs Gleichnus aus derselbigen Zeit, wo d'Viecher noh hab'n red'n künná. Aus uralten, vierhundert- bis sechshundertjährigen Büchern neu in die Welt gestellt für die österreichischen Landsleute" dienten Goethes „Reineke Fuchs", aber auch die alten Texte des Reinaert und des Reinke de vos. N. gelang es dabei nicht nur, den niederösterr. Bauerndialekt, sondern auch die gesamte bäuerliche Anschauungswelt des Neunkirchner Raumes lebendig darzustellen. Gem. mit Zeidler begründete N. außerdem die vierbändige „Deutsch-österreichische Literaturgeschichte", die später von Castle fortgesetzt wurde. Überdies befaßte sich N. mit Stud. über den niederösterr. Bauernstand, von denen er einige im Selbstverlag veröff.
</Haupttext>
<Werke>W.: Da Roanad. Grammatik des niederösterr. Dialekts, 1886; Der Fuchs Roáner . . ., 1889, 2. Aufl. 1909; Vokalismus der bayr.-österr. Mundart, 1895; Geograph. Namenkde., in: Die Erdkde. 18, 1903; Dt. Sprachlehre . . ., 1905, 2. Aufl. 1906; etc. Hrsg.: Dt. Mundarten, 1896 ff.; Dt.-österr. Literaturgeschichte, 4 Bde., gem. mit J. Zeidler und E. Castle, 1899-1937.
</Werke>
<Literatur>L.: RP vom 2. und 11. 5. 1916, 27. 7. und 15. 8. 1918; Wr. Ztg. und N. Fr. Pr. vom 26. 7. 1918; Z. für österr. Volkskde., Jg. 3, 1897, S. 319, Jg. 4, 1898, S. 52; Monatsbl. des Ver. für Landeskde. von NÖ, Jg. 17, 1918, S. 190 ff.; Petermanns Mitt., 1918, S. 228; Unsere Heimat, NF, Bd. 11, 1938, S. 200 ff.; I. M. Swift Peacock, Der grammat. Anhang J. W. N.s „Fuchs Roánad" im Vergleich mit dem heute lebendigen Wortschatz in der Mundart der Gemeinde Hafning, Bez. Neunkirchen, NÖ, phil. Diss. Wien, 1969;

```
Giebisch-Gugitz; Kosel; Rollett, Neue Beitrr., Tl. 10, 1898, S. 80; Kosch, Das kath. Deutschland; Wer ist's? 1905-14.
  </Literatur>
      <Autor>(M. Hornung)
  </Autor>
      <PubInfo Reihe="ÖBL 1815-1950" Band="7" Lieferung="31" Seite="21" Jahr="1976" Monat="" Tag="">ÖBL 1815-1950, Bd. 7 (Lfg. 31, 1976), S. 21</PubInfo>
    </Lexikonartikel>
  </Eintrag>
```


Excerpt of the dbo@ema entry of Johann Willibald Nagl:


```
<database name="dboe_1">
  <table name="person">
    <column name="id">12102</column>
    <column name="vorname">Johann Willibald</column>
    <column name="nachname">Nagl</column>
    <column name="gebTag">11</column>
    <column name="gebMonat">5</column>
    <column name="gebJahr">1856</column>
    <column name="gebOrt">Natschbach b. Neunkirchen, NÖ</column>
    <column name="gebOrt_id">7082</column>
    <column name="todTag">23</column>
    <column name="todMonat">7</column>
    <column name="todJahr">1918</column>
    <column name="todOrt">Diepolz b. Neunkirchen, NÖ</column>
    <column name="todOrt_id">NULL</column>
    <column name="geschlecht">2</column>
    <column name="adresse"></column>
    <column name="plz">-1</column>
    <column name="ort"></column>
    <column name="email"></column>
    <column name="tel1"></column>
    <column name="tel2"></column>
    <column name="tel3"></column>
    <column name="adressverlauf"></column>
    <column name="verwandschaft">Mutter: --- Geburtsdatum: --- Todesdatum: --- Anm.: --- (bereits in Datenbank: ja/nein) Vater: --- Geburtsdatum:--- Todesdatum: --- Anm.: --- (bereits in Datenbank: ja/nein) Gattin/Gatte: --- Geburtsdatum: --- Todesdatum: --- Anm.: --- (bereits in Datenbank: ja/nein) Weitere Verwandte: --- Anm./Verweise: ---
  </column>
  <column name="kontaktperson"></column>
          <column name="ausbildung">Regierungsrat Dr.phil. Schule: Universität --- Ort: --- von: --- bis: --- Anm: Theologie; abgebrochen --- Schule: Universität --- Ort: Wien --- von: --- bis: 1886 --- Anm: Phil. und Germanistik; 1886 Dr.phil. --- Schule: --- Ort: --- von: --- bis: --- Anm: --- Beruf: Lehrer --- Ort: --- von: --- bis: --- Anm: an verschiedenen Schulen --- Beruf: Priv. Dozent für Mundartforschung --- Ort: Universität Wien --- von: --- bis: --- Anm: --- Beruf: Schriftsteller --- Ort: --- von: --- bis: --- Anm: --- Beruf: Herausgeber der Zeitschrift „Deutsche Mundarten" --- Ort: --- von: --- bis: --- Anm: --- Beruf: --- Ort: --- von: --- bis: --- Anm: --- Ehrenamtl. Tätigkeiten:</column>
  </table>
</database>
```

A Multiform Balanced Dependency Treebank for Romanian

Mihaela Colhon
University of Craiova
Department of Informatics
Craiova, Romania
mcolhon@gmail.com

Cătălina Mărănduc
"Al. I. Cuza" University,
Iasi, Romania
Institute of Linguistics
"Iorgu Iordan Al. Rosetti"
Bucharest, Romania
catalinamaranduc@gmail.com

Cătălin Mititelu
Bucharest
Romania
catalinmititelu@yahoo.com

Abstract

The UAIC-RoDia-DepTb is a balanced treebank, containing texts in non-standard language: 2,575 chats sentences, old Romanian texts (a Gospel printed in 1648, a codex of laws printed in 1818, a novel written in 1910), regional popular poetry, legal texts, Romanian and foreign fiction, quotations. The proportions are comparable; each of these types of texts is represented by subsets of at least 1,000 phrases, so that the parser can be trained on their peculiarities. The annotation of the treebank started in 2007, and it has classical tags, such as those in school grammar, with the intention of using the resource for didactic purposes. The classification of circumstantial modifiers is rich in semantic information. We present in this paper the development in progress of this resource which has been automatically annotated and entirely manually corrected. We try to add new texts, and to make it available in more formats, by keeping all the morphological and syntactic information annotated, and adding logical-semantic information. We will describe here two conversions, from the classic syntactic format into Universal Dependencies format and into a logical-semantic layer, which will be shortly presented.

1 Introduction

The annotation of UAIC-RoDia DepTb[1] was started in 2007, prompted by the need to complete the lack of corpora for Romanian with a high degree of annotated data. The creator, Augusto Perez, 2014, used classical tags with the intention to use the treebank for teaching purposes, in preparing students for exams.

Since then, there have created more resources and processing tools. Their creators are all interested in standard contemporary language, overlooking the complex structures, the originality of expression. Their aim is to obtain superior accuracy by processing simple texts. A big corpus for contemporary standard language (CoRoLA) has been created (Tufiș et al., 1998). It includes publications obtained from editors, spoken language and also a treebank consisting of 9,500 sentences, affiliated with the UD (Universal Dependencies) group. UAIC-RoDepTb is a balanced corpus, having more styles. We contribute our 4,500 sentences, which are in contemporary standard language, to the Romanian Treebank affiliated with UD.

However, the UD group includes all kinds of Treebanks, balanced, or containing old languages, Social Media, and so on. The initial purpose of this group was to build a universal parser. The common features of all the languages have been highlighted, admitting the peculiarities only as sub-classifications that can be taken into consideration or not, according to the user's wish. More and more treebanks for over 30 languages have been affiliated. The uniformity of the flexible annotation format has created the possibility of multiple alignments, useful in Machine Translation and comparative language studies.

UAIC-RoDia DepTb can participate to this project as another treebank, for non-standard Romanian. Our Treebank has now 19,825 sentences in progress, in the UAIC classic syntactic convention of annotation. If we subtract the 4,500 sentences already introduced into the UD, there remain 15,325 sentences to be transposed in UD conventions: 2,575 sentences from chat, 1,230

[1]UAIC-RoDia = ISLRN 156-635-615-024-0

Proceedings of Knowledge Resources for the Socio-Economic Sciences and Humanities associated with RANLP-17, pages 9–18,
Varna, Bulgaria, 7 Sep 2017.

from regional folk poetry, 6,882 in Old Romanian, a Gospel published in 1648 and a codex of laws issued in 1818, Romanian fiction, a novel by Matthew Caragiale *The Princes of Old Palace*, written in 1910, and 3,894 quotations from the thesaurus dictionary or its bibliography, containing poetry by known authors, too. The section already introduced in UD contains fragments from the Romanian version of Orwell's *1984* novel, sentences from the Aquis Communitaire laws, from Wikipedia in Romanian, and from the Frame Net (Baker et al., 1998), translated in Romanian. The sentences with complex structure have not been avoided, neither have short, elliptical ones. The average frequency is high, some sub-corpora have 25-29 words per sentence, and the general average frequency is 19.91 words per sentence.

The differences between the UAIC annotation conventions and UD ones have been shown in previous work (Mărănduc and Perez, 2015), (Mititelu et al., 2015). Shortly, it's about the annotation of functional words, considered in UAIC as heads, such as the copulative verbs, while in UD they are subordinated, and another convention for the annotation of coordination. Also, UAIC treebank has the same tag to mark a relation expressed by a word or by a subordinate clause, and UD use tags as: *ccomp*, *csubj*, *advcl* where the first *c* or the last *cl* means *clause*.

The annotation in the UAIC conventions was not renounced, for reasons of continuity. There has also been created an Old-Ro-POS-tagger for the complete morphological analysis of Old Romanian (starting with the sixteenth century) (Mărănduc et al., 2017b). This classic, annotated with rich information format can be considered as the pivot from which the other two formats have to be automatically obtained.

The logical-semantic format that is actually used to capitalize the semantic information present in syntactic and morphological UAIC-RoDepTb annotations is described in Mărănduc et al. (2017a). It has similarities with the Tectogrammatic layer of the Prague Dependency Treebank (PDT) (Bohmová et al., 2003) and Abstract Meaning Representation (AMR) (Bănărescu et al., 2013).

In this paper, we briefly describe the semantic format, showing how most classic-syntactic tags can be automatically transformed into semantic ones. Some of the syntactic tags are highly ambiguous from the semantic point of view, and they are manually transformed using an interface that has drop-down lists (Hociung, 2016).

We will describe a program called TREEOPS that automatically transforms non-ambiguous syntactic tags. We shall give examples of rules for the transformation of syntactic into semantic tags, and then, we shall give examples of rules written in the same program, for transforming the UAIC syntactic structure of trees into the UD one.

2 Related Work

2.1 Dependency Treebanks

The UAIC-RoDia DepTb is annotated in Dependency Grammar, a flexible formalism founded by Tesnière (1959), Kern (1883) and actualized as Functional Dependency Grammar by Tapanainen and Jarvinen (1998), Mel'čuk (1988). Actually, a big number of corpora in the world have adopted the same formalism. All these corpora exist only if the work is going on; if they grow organically, if they have the flexibility to change their format into another, adopted by more universal resources, and the creators always try to introduce more refined annotations of linguistic phenomena. Otherwise, the amount of annotated information or of texts introduced is exceeded by other resources, and the format becomes obsolete, difficult to compare with the new modern ones. Consequently, the users forget this resource and prefer another.

In 2003, the PDT authors described the three level structure of their treebank and the Tectogrammatic level (that includes semantic, logical and syntactic information) (Bohmová et al., 2003). The PDT authors publish their updates every two years (Bejček et al., 2013). They have for a long time been interested in semantics and its links with syntax (Sgall et al., 1986).

BulTreeBank is another big member of the UD community. This treebank has been previously annotated in the HPSG grammar and automatically transposed into Dependency formalism. The authors are also interested in semantics (Simov and Osenova, 2011).

For the PENN Treebank, the third version was available in 1999 (Marcus et al., 1999). Actually, this treebank is also involved in semantics research or in the annotation of entities and events (Song et al., 2015).

2.2 Semantic Annotations

In the UAIC NLP group, about 1,000 sentences from the English FrameNet have been translated in Romanian (Trandabăţ, 2010). Retaining the semantic annotation from the English FrameNet, the author has made a first set of semantic annotations on Romanian sentences. Just as the English FrameNet (Baker et al., 1998), these annotations only cover the core structure of the sentence, called Semantic Frame.

The similarities between the system of semantic annotations presented here and the AMR (Abstract Meaning Representation) logical categories (Bănărescu et al., 2013) are obvious. However, there are also important differences, since the resulting graph of the AMR semantic annotation is not a dependency tree, and the nodes are not words, but concepts.

The similitudes with the Tectogrammatic layer of the PDT (Prague Dependency Treebank) are more important. They also have, like in our semantic system, categories for annotating the semantic information existing in the exclamatory, or interrogative form of the sentence, in the modality and the tense of verbs, considering the punctuation or morphological annotation as containing semantic information.

3 The UAIC-RoDepTb Logical-Semantic Format

3.1 Short Characterization of the UAIC Semantic Format

The circumstantial information gives us indications about the state of communication: succession in time, past, future, space: TEMP, PAST, FTR, LOC, or information regarding logical relationships: cause, purpose, consequence, opposition, concession, condition, exception, cumulation, association, reference, restriction, result: CAUS, PURP, CSQ, OPPOS, CNCS, COND, EXCP, CUMUL, ASSOC, REFR, RESTR, RSLT, respectively.

Information on the names of objects or actors is derived from the classification of the pronouns: Appurtenance, Deictic, Emphatic, Undefined: APP, DX, IDENT, UNDEF. The classification of the functional words (considered as connectors) give us a classification of relations. There are six types of connectors: CNADVS, CNCNCL, CNCONJ, CNDISJ, CNSBRD, CNCOP, the first four being coordinating connectors, the fifth being subordinating connector, and the last being the copulative verb *"to be"*, considered as connector between the subject and their description rendered by the predicative noun. As a logical point of view, the different type of connectors mark relations of inclusion, reunion, disjunction, intersection, particularization or generalization of properties, between the set of things which the linguistic signs refer to. The truth value of sentences par rapport to the real World can also be established, and it receives modal values such as: existence, possibility and necessity.

There is also information regarding the reality of the action: optative, uncertain, potentiality, generic, dynamic: OPTV, UNCTN, POTN, GNR, DYN. Five quantifiers are considered: necessity, possibility, existence, universality, and negation: QNECES, QPOSSIB, QEXIST, QUNIV, QNEG. Other information qualifies the type of the communication: addressee, blame, greeting, politeness, interrogative, exclamatory, incidence: ADDR, BLAM, GREET, POLIT, INTROG, EXCL, INCID, respectively. The last tag marks the change of the emitter and receiver roles, i.e. it marks another communication state; the first and the second persons refer to other characters in the INCID text, isolated by NOAPP punctuation, than in the rest of the sentence. This is very important for a future program that would automatically establish the co-references. Also this information about the communication state is important for future pragmatics research.

EQUIVHEAD is the mark for the ellipsis. This mark allows a connector or punctuation element to represent a copy of the meaning of its head and to have dependents with a similar, and symmetrical structure. The expletive is classified according to the value it repeats: EXPL:BEN, EXPL:EXPR, EXPL:OBJ, EXLP:DFND, EXPL:PAT, EXPL:RCPR, EXPL:APP, EXPL:EXP. This annotation is also in view of a future program that would automatically establish the co-references.

The punctuation elements also have a semantic value in our system. The semantic value of punctuation elements is shown in Druguş (2015). The final ones are marks for the form: INTROG, EXCL, END. The non-final are annotated as CNCONJ if they mark the coordination, or NOAPP (non-appurtenance) if they are subordinated to an INCID, ADDR or interjection (ALERT, IMIT,

Judgment	nsubj	dobj	npred	other
Process	ACT	RSLT	-	-
Performance	PERFR	PERF	QLF	-
Actantial	ACT	PAT	-	BEN
Experience	EXPR	EXP	-	BEN
Comunic.	EMT	CTNT	-	RCPT
Definition	DFND	-	DFNS	CNCOP
Chang.idnt	DFND	-	DFNS	CNCOP
Characteriz	CTNT	-	QLF	CNCOP
Existence	QEXIST	-	-	LOC,TIME

Table 1: The semantic roles depending on the type of judgment.

AFF) head. The others are markers of dislocation (topical changes, frequent in Old Romanian) or elaboration (structures providing additional information that can be omitted): DISL, ELAB.

Finally, since not all sentences contain events, we have made a classification of the types of scenarios that govern the roles in the sentence (see Table 1 3.1).

3.2 Syntactic Relations Without Semantic Ambiguity

The classical syntactic format of the UAIC-RoDepTb has 14 kinds of circumstantial modifiers, carefully supervised by linguists. Actually, the time and space automatic annotation is at the core of the computational linguists interest; our corpus can be a useful training corpus for future automatic parsing of the communication situation circumstances. The second edition of the workshop on "*Corpus-based Research in the Humanities*" (CRH) Viena, January 25th-26th 2018, will have a special topic concerning time and space annotation in textual data.[2] The annotation of the time and space is semi-automatically rendered; the circumstantial modifiers are automatically annotated, but words with the same meaning can have syntactic ambiguous values, as nominal modifier or prepositional object, and must be manually annotated.

Besides the circumstantials, other syntactic relations that can be transposed in a unique semantic tag are: *superl.*, "*superlative*", "*=SUPER*", *comp.*, "*comparative*","*=COMP*", *ap.*, "*apposition*", *=RSMP*, *incid.*, "*incident*", *=INCID*, *neg.*, "*negation*", *QNEG*, *voc.*, "*vocative*", *=ADDR*, *c.ag.*, "*agent complement*", *=ACT*. Our classical syntactic tagset has 44 relations; having 14 circumstantials and the 7 relations above, it results that almost half of them (21) are semantically monovalent. This is a consequence of the fact that the classic format contains a lot of semantic information.

3.3 Syntactic Relations with Semantic Ambiguity

Besides the relationships with a single semantic interpretation, it is also possible to make automatic transformations by rules with more conditions, using morphological information or word lemma. Examples:

- The syntactic tag *det.* can be transposed in the semantic tag DX "*Deixis*", if the morphological analysis (POS-tag) begins with Td "*Demonstrative article*", or in the semantic tag UNDEF, if the POS-tag begins with Ti "*undefined article*", or in the semantic tag DEF if the morphological analysis begins with Tf "*definite article*", or in the semantic tag APP "*appurtenance*" if the morphological analysis begins with Ts "*possessive article*".

- The syntactic tag *aux.* "*auxiliary*" can be transposed in the following semantic tags: OPTV or PAST, if the form of the auxiliary (and of the conjugate verb) indicate(s) the verbal conditional or the past tense, FTR, if the auxiliary is *vrea* "*will*" or PASS "*passive*".

For similar situations, the tags can be automatically transposed from the syntactic format into the semantic one by writing rules with two or three conditions in the TREEOPS program (see below).

3.4 Syntactic Tags Semantically Polyvalent

Syntactic relations classified by morphological criteria, such as: a.subst. (noun attribute), a.vb. (verbal attribute), c.prep. (prepositional complement), have a great semantic ambiguity, and so do those in the Table 1, the column 2 and 3 They can have almost any semantic value. We automatically modify the monovalent relations, for which we write rules with one condition. Other relationships that depend on several factors need rules with more conditions, and the structure of the trees, too. TREEOPS makes all the changes

[2] http://www.oeaw.ac.at/ac/crh2/

which are not ambiguous, in accordance with the rules introduced, and the ambiguous relations remain unchanged (as syntactic tags). At this moment, they are manually changed by an expert, simultaneously with supervising automatic annotations. In this way, we are building the training corpus for a semantic parser, see (Aho and Ullman, 1972). The training corpus has now 5,025 sentences in Old Romanian and 1,130 sentences in Contemporary Romanian; we must increase and balance it, adding approximately 3,500 sentences in Contemporary Romanian.

We will use a statistical semantic parser. It will receive the documents having all the possible automatically processed transformations (consequently having mixed syntactic and semantic relations), and will statistically transform the syntactic ambiguous ones into semantic relations. It will be similar to a mixed parser, first the rules written in the TREEOPS program will be applied, to make the transformations non-ambiguous, and then the parser will receive the output of TREEOPS program (that are correct since the resulting from the supervised syntactic layer) so as to solve statistically the ambiguous syntactic relations.

The supervision of the automatic transformation simultaneously with the manual choice of semantic values for the ambiguous syntactic relations is performed currently by using an interface called Treebank Annotator (Hociung, 2016) that has drop-down lists for each feature in each of the three formats: UAIC, UD and semantic. The format is selected from a list of options before opening a document.

4 The TREEOPS Program. Rules for Transformations

4.1 Presentation of the Program

The automatic transformations are done using a tool called TREEOPS. It is an all purpose rule-based XML transformer, i.e. it is able to produce a new XML structure, having an XML as input and using a customized set of rules. It defines a new simple language for XML transformations, where each rule is described by the following pattern:

selector => **action**

During a transforming process the XML is traversed node by node and the TREEOPS rule is converted into an *if-then* statement as follows:

if (**selector** *matches* `node`) *then* **action**

TREEOPS requires the **selector** to be an XML Path Language[3] (XPath) expression and the **action** an internal defined action that can take parameters, as is, for example, `changeAttrValue(<new_value>)` which changes the value of the current XML attribute. In fact, TREEOPS uses the power of the XSLT language by transforming the set of rules into an XSLT template that will be applied to the input file to obtain the new desired structure.

For example, the rule defined as:

```
//word[@deprel='superl.']/@deprel =>
    changeAttrValue('SUPER')
```

becomes an XSLT template:

```
<xsl:template match="//word[@deprel='
    superl.']/@deprel">
<xsl:call-template name="changeAttrValue
    ">
<xsl:with-param name="new_value" select=
    "'SUPER'"/>
</xsl:call-template>
</xsl:template>
```

where the `changeAttrValue` template is predefined as:

```
<xsl:template name="changeAttrValue">
<xsl:param name="new_value"/>
<xsl:attribute name="{name(.)}">
<xsl:value-of select="$new_value"/>
</xsl:attribute>
</xsl:template>
```

4.2 Rules for the Transposition of Classical Syntactic Format into Semantic One

For the 21 tags with a unique semantic value, we have written 21 rules with a unique condition. Example: the rule below transforms the negation into a logical quantifier:

```
//word[@deprel='neg.']/@deprel =>
    changeAttrValue('QNEG')
```

The rule exemplified below has two conditions. It changes the syntactic value coord. in a connector for the reunion. We classified the coordination relations in four logical categories, taking into account the lemma of the coordinating conjunction: reunion (CNCONJ), adversative (QNADVS) (opposition where the related entities do not exclude

[3]`https://www.w3.org/TR/xpath/`

each other), disjunction (QNDISJ i.e. exclusion, and conclusive. The other three are written in the same way.

```
//word[@deprel='coord.' and (@lemma='şi'
    or @lemma='nici')]/@deprel =>
   changeAttrValue('CNCONJ')
```

To give an example for a rule with three conditions, the rule of the PAST relationship attribution depends on the aux. syntactic relation, the word form of the auxiliary, and the postag of the main verb form, being a compound time. The information needed has been previously annotated in the syntactic format.

```
//word[@deprel='aux.' and (@form='am' or
    @form='ai' or @form='aţi' or @form
    ='a' or @form='au') and following-
    sibling::word [@postag='Vmp'or
    @postag='Vap']]/@deprel =>
   changeAttrValue('PAST')
```

4.3 Rules for the Transposition of Classical Syntactic Format into UD Format

To transpose the classic syntactic format into UD conventions, we have formulated another set of rules in a similar way. Here's an example of a rule with one condition:

```
//word[@deprel='c.prep.']/@deprel =>
   changeAttrValue('nmod:pmod')
```

As a general observation, in the first case, we need to transpose a syntactic tag set of 44 classes into a semantic tag set of 95, so more conditions have to be done and more cases remain to be manually solved. On the other hand, the transposition of the UAIC syntactic tag set of 44 tags into the UD tagset of 28 common tags is a simpler operation, based on unifications. Of course, these transformations will also need to be supervised.

5 Structural Transformations of Trees

We decided that the structural transformations should be applied both to obtain the UD format and also to the semantic format, to make it more accessible to alignments or comparisons with other treebanks. The subordination of prepositions was a structural change also applied to the PDT Tectogrammatic layer. Establishing relationships between meaningful (also called self-semantic) words is more appropriate for the semantic analysis of the sentence.

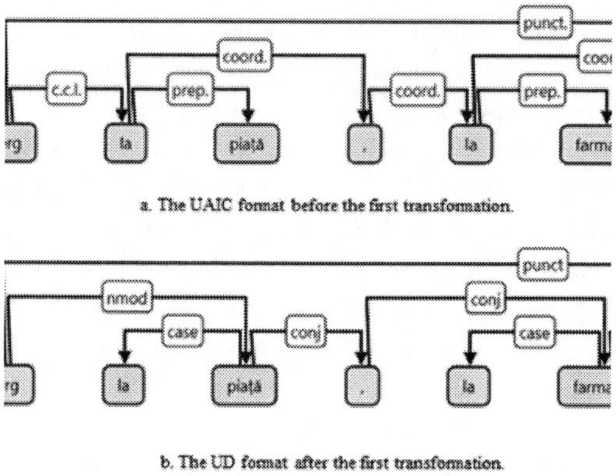

Figure 1: "*To the market, to the pharmacy*" before and after the subordination of prepositions.

5.1 Subordination of the Relational Words to the Word Which It Introduces

The subordination of prepositions to the word which they are introducing is the simplest and most frequent of the operations. The order of the operations is not random. Being the most common, usually located at the tree leaves, it must be the first transformation.

The rule for the first transformation is described in pseudocode in listing 1 and the result can be seen in Figure 1.

Listing 1: Transformation 1

```
if word1[@id="x", @postag="Sp*"] and
   word2[@head="x"]
then
  word1/@head ← word2/@id
  word2/@head ← word1/@head
  foreach remaining wordN[@head="x"]
    wordN/@head ← word2/@id
```

The subordination of relational words which introduce the subordinated sentence is similar to the first; the aim is to subordinate the relational words in a complex sentence. This rule must be applied after the first one, because it is no longer applied to the leaves, but to the upper structure of the tree.

The rule is almost the same: if there is a word1 with the id="x" and the postag="Cs*", or "Pw*", or "Rw*", or "Qs" and a word2 with head="x" (usually the next word), then change the head of word1 with the id of word2 and the head of word2 with the head of word1.

If the subordinate word is a relative pronoun preceded by a preposition, then the preposition has already been subordinated to it by the first transformation. Consequently, we must introduce a restriction of the type with *the head="x" and without the postag="Sp*"*, because we search for another subordinate word, which is the head of a subtree.

A disadvantage of the UAIC annotation convention is that there is no information about the syntactic relationship of the relative pronouns and adverbs in the subordinated sentence, but only about their role in the complex sentence. Therefore, they can only get the tag mark, obtained by automatically changing the subord. relationship..

A human annotator must specify their function in the subordinate sentence, because the relative pronoun, adjective and adverb are not marks. Sometimes the relative pronoun is a nominal modifier in the subordinate sentence, and then its automatic subordination to the head of the subordinate sentence by the transformation 2 is erroneous and will be manually corrected.

5.2 Subordination of the Copulative Verb and of the Subject to the Predicative Noun

This transformation has the aim of swapping the places of the copulative verb and the predicative noun, in the cases where the copulative verb is the verb "to be". In the UAIC conventions of annotation, there are other 9 verbs annotated as copulative. Their predicative nouns becomes *xcomp* in the UD convention.

This transformation has the advantage that it establishes an equivalence between the structure of dependencies of the nominal predicate and the passive voice, which is also built with the verb "to be", subordinated to the verbal participle, which formally resembles an adjective predicative noun (and it has the same number and gender with the subject).

This transformation is as follows: if there is a word with id="x", and lemma="fi", and postag="Vm*" and head="q" (and if there is a word with id="y", head="x", and deprel="sbj.")[4] and if there is a word with the id="z", head="x" and deprel="n.pred.", then the word with deprel="n.pred." changes head="q" and the word with id="x" changes head="z" and the word with id="y" changes head="z". The deprel="n.pred." is changed with the deprel of the word with

[4]No mandatory condition, because in Romanian the subject is usually understood.

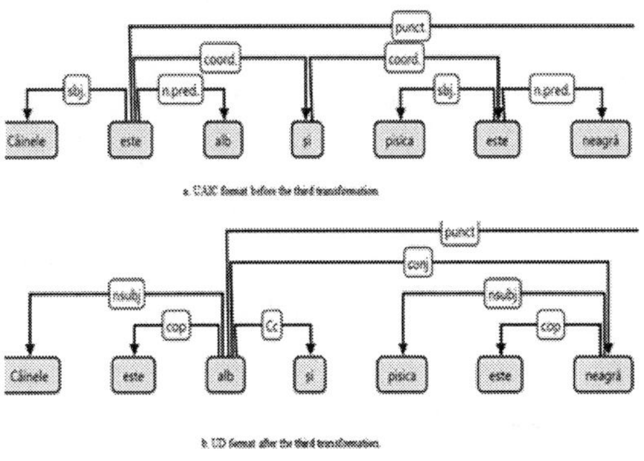

Figure 2: The UAIC format before and the UD one after the subordination of the copulative verb: "*The dog is white and the cat is black.*"

lemma="fi", and this one take the deprel CNCOP.

A general condition must be observed for all the rules: If the id of the head changes, then all the other words having the changed head must also change their head. Therefore, the dependencies of the copulative verb "to be" become dependencies to the predicative noun, i.e. they change the head="x" in head="z" For this rule, the exception are the words with morphological analysis (POS-tag) Qn, aux., Qs.(see Figure 2).

5.3 Subordination of all Coordinated Elements to the First One

In the UAIC convention, the coordination is rendered by an asymmetrical tree, also having as head the first element, but each coordinating element (word with full meaning, functional word or punctuation) being subordinated to the element above and acting as the head of the element below. Similarly with the subordinated elements of relation considered as heads, the coordination elements also are heads and are positioned between the related elements.

Consequently, in the new conception, the relational words for the coordination must be subordinated to the meaningful words which they introduce, by a rule similarly formulated as the first rule in the 5.1 chapter.

Then, all the coordinated meaningful words must be subordinated to the first one. A rule for retaining the previous head is added, because in a sentence with more coordination relations they must be subordinate to the first element of their chain, and not to another one.

The elements with the deprel="coord.", and the

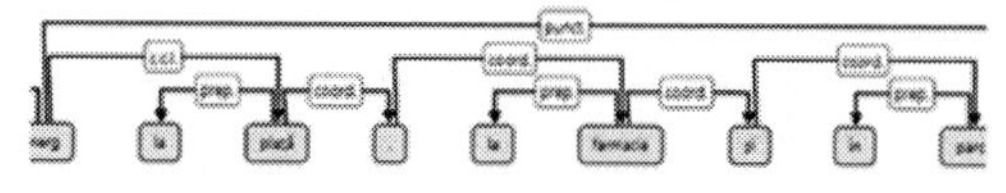

a. The UAIC annotation before the fourth transformation.

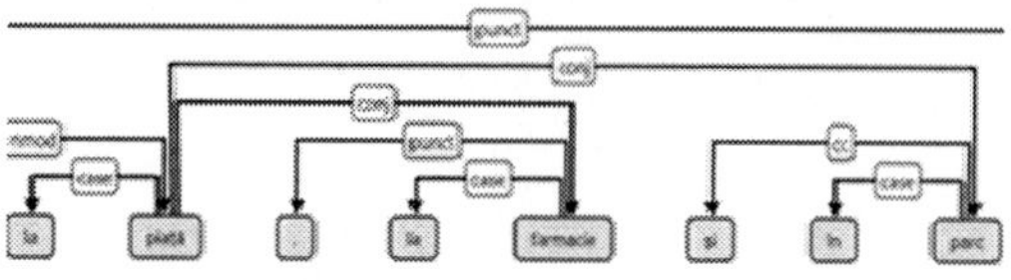

b. The UD convention after the fourth transformation.

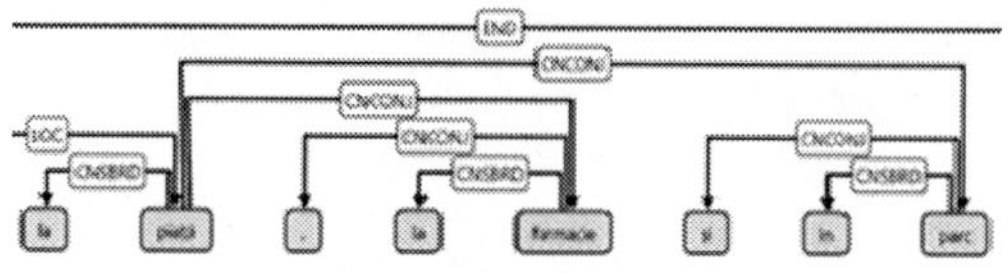

c. The Semantic convention after the fourth transformation.

Figure 3: The UAIC format before, the UD and the Semantic format after the transformation of the coordination: *"Go to the market, to the pharmacy and in the park."*

postag="COMMA", are also subordinated to the meaningful word which they coordinate. Simultaneously, the deprels of all these words change, differently in UD and in the Semantic annotation.

The result of this transformation is shown in Figure 3)

As can be seen, in Figure 3 and 4 3 the transformation of relational words and of the copulative verb has already been made.

Coordination in sentences takes place between long-distance elements. Because it acts in the top of the tree, this transformation must be applied after all the others.

In Figure 4, the following text is annotated in two conventions:

"I think that there will come some days of effort that will pass, that we will escape and that we will be happy."

The results of applying the other transformations can be seen in the figure 4 a: First, the preposition de "of" has been subordinated to the noun "effort". Secondly, the conjunction "că" ("that"). repeated three times, and the relative pronoun "care" ("which") have been subordinated to the head of the subordinate sentences. Then, the predicative noun "fericiți" ("happy") is the head for the copulative verb.

Finally, the "ccomp" sentences 2 and 3 have been subordinated to the first one, and the comma and the conjunction "și" ("and"), the two connectors of the three coordinate sentences, are subordinated of the closest coordinated element on the left. (see Figure 4).

The rules for the transformations have been all formulated in the same way of the listening in the 3.1 chapter.

6 Conclusions and Future Works

Transforming UAIC-RoDepTb so that it can be used in multiple future applications and can be compared to similar corpora is one of our priorities.

TREEOPS, the program described in this paper (section 4) is a very important tool. It is language independent. For any resource in XML format to be transformed, another set of rules can be written, depending on the original format and on the one in which it is intended to be transformed, regardless of the language. As we have shown above, format flexibility is very important for all resources, so they can always be compatible with newer resources created in more modern formats. The TREEOPS program does not have a variant for CONLLU, but we have transformation programs from XML to CONLLU and vice versa. TREEOPS has been successfully tested to transform the classic format of our UAIC treebank into the semantic format, we will begin testing TREEOPS for the conversion from classical UAIC to the UD format; after completion, the program will be available on the Sourceforge page. [5] The evaluation of the accuracy is in progress. It is difficult to evaluate it, because the program does not transform all the semantic structure, but only the non ambiguous relation; the manual transformation of the ambiguous one should not be evaluated as a decrease in the accuracy of the conversion program.

Another important task is to ensure optimal digitization of the old Romanian language information, starting with its first attestations. Digitization does not only mean scanning old manuscripts and prints to avoid their disappearance with paper damage, but also reading the data contained in them.

For this, a very useful tool has been created and, for the first time ever, seventeenth-century

[5]https://sourceforge.net/

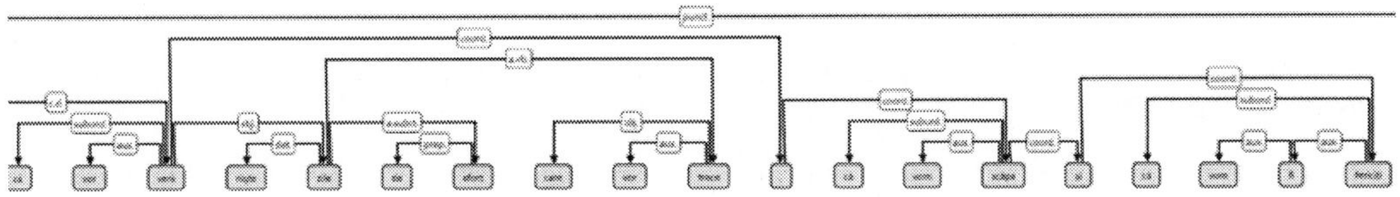

a. The UAIC format before the fourth transformation.

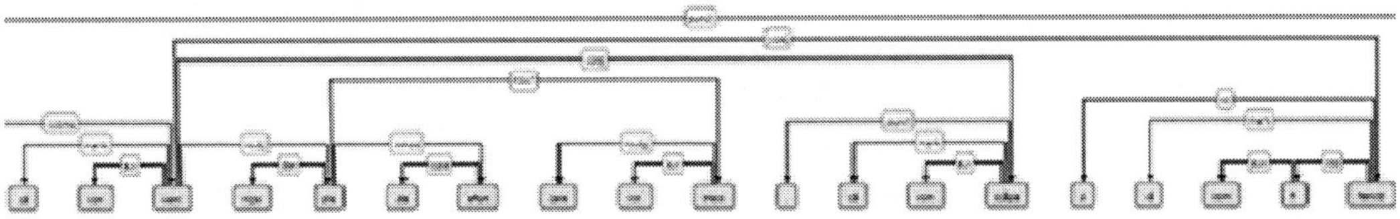

b. The UD format after all the four transformations.

Figure 4: The transformation of the coordination applied at the top of the tree, after all the other structural transformations

Cyrillic Romanian letters have been made editable by an optical character recognizer (OCR) built in Chisinau (Colesnicov et al., 2016), (Cojocaru et al., 2017).

Another important tool is the OldRoPOS-tagger (Mărănduc et al., 2017b), which provides the first level of annotation of the texts obtained after their transliteration into Latin characters. In order to syntactically parse these texts with many particularities, especially related to the very free order of the words and subordinate sentences, a continuous training of the syntactic parser is needed.

By creating the converter described in this article, we will transfer all these sentences in the UD and Semantic format. The operation is under way. Transformations will be supervised and the rules for the conversions improved.

We also aim to include the oldest *New Testament* (Alba Iulia 1648) in the project *Pragmatic Resources in Old Indo-European Languages* (PROIEL), that is part of the Universal Dependencies (UD) group, and align the oldest *New Testaments* in Latin, Greek, Armenian, Slavonic. The philological studies of old translations and the etymological studies can benefit from the alignment of the first printed Romanian New Testament in this project. The first part of the *New Testament* (1648), the *Gospel*, was introduced in the classic syntactic format and in the semantic one. We also have to introduce the second part, the *Acts of the Apostles*.

Since the UAIC-UD transformation does not require the introduction of new syntactic relationships, we do not believe that we need to build a syntactic parser on the UD format. A parser for Contemporary Romanian in UD format has been created (Mititelu and Irimia, 2015), and we can train it on Old Romanian, too.

Once a large training corpus has been built in the semantic format, we will create a semantic parser. The semantic parser will complete the set of tools for processing old Romanian.

References

Alfred V. Aho and Jeffrey D. Ullman. 1972. *The Theory of Parsing, Translation and Compiling*, volume 1. Prentice-Hall, Englewood Cliffs, NJ.

Collin F. Baker, Charles J. Fillmore, and John B. Lowe. 1998. The berkeley framenet project. In *Proceedings of the COLING-ACL*. Montreal Canada.

Eduard Bejček, Eva Hajičová, Jan Hajič, P. Jínová, Vaclava Kettnerová, Veronika Kolářová, Marie Mikulová, Jiri Mírovský, Anna Nedoluzhko, Jamila Panevová, Lucie Poláková, Magda Ševčíková, J. Štěpánek, and Sarka Zikánová. 2013. *Prague Dependency Treebank 3.0. Data/software*. Univerzita Karlova v Praze, Prague.

Alena Bohmová, Jan Hajič, Eva Hajičova, and Barbora Hladka. 2003. *The Prague Dependency Treebank: A Three-Level Annotation Scenario. Text, Speech and Language Technology*. Springer Publisher, Prague.

Laura Bănărescu, Claire Bonial, Shu Cai, Mădălina Georgescu, Kira Griffitt, Ulf Hermjakob, Kevin Knight, Philip Koehn, Martha Palmer, and Nathan Schneider. 2013. Abstract meaning representation for sembanking. In *Proceedings of the 7th Linguistic Annotation Workshop and Interoperability with Discourse*. pages 178–186.

Svetlana Cojocaru, Alexander Colesnicov, and Ludmila Malahova. 2017. Digitization of old romanian texts printed in the cyrillic script. In *Proceedings of International Conference on Digital Access to Textual Cultural Heritage*. pages 143–148.

Alexandru Colesnicov, Ludmila Malahov, and Tudor Bumbu. 2016. Digitization of romanian printed texts of the 17th century. In *Proceedings of the 12th International Conference Linguistic Resources and Tools for Processing the Romanian Language*. Alexandru Ioan Cuza University Press, pages 1–11.

Ioachim Druguş. 2015. Metalingua: a metalanguage for the semantic annotation of natural languages. In *Proceedings of the 11th International Conference Linguistic Resources and Tools for Processing the Romanian Language*. Alexandru Ioan Cuza University Press, pages 79–94.

Florinel Hociung. 2016. *Treebank Annotator - disertation*. Faculty of Computer Science, Alexandru Ioan Cuza University, Iaşi.

Franz Kern. 1883. *Zur Methodik des deutschen Unterrichts*. Nicolaische Verlags-Buch-handlung, Berlin.

Cătălina Mărănduc and Cenel-Augusto Perez. 2015. A romanian dependency treebank. *International Journal of Computational Linguistics and Applications* 6(2):25–40.

Cătălina Mărănduc, Monica Mihaela Rizea, and Dan Cristea. 2017a. Mapping dependency relations onto semantic categories. In *Proceedings of the International Conference on Computational Linguistics and Intelligent Text Processing (CICLing)*.

Cătălina Mărănduc, Radu Simionescu, and Dan Cristea. 2017b. Hybrid pos-tagger for old romanian. In *Proceedings of the International Conference on Computational Linguistics and Intelligent Text Processing (CICLing)*.

Mitchell P. Marcus, Beatrice Santorini, Mary Ann Marcinkiewicz, and Ann Taylor. 1999. Ldc.upenn treebank 3. In *Tehnical Repport*. University of Pennsylvania, pages 1–230.

Igor Mel'čuk. 1988. *Dependency Syntax: Theory and Practice*. The SUNY Press, Albany, NY.

Verginica Mititelu, Cătălina Mărănduc, and Elena Irimia. 2015. Universal and language-specific dependency relations for analyzing romanian. In *Proceedings of the Third International Conference on Dependency Linguistics, Depling*. Uppsala University, pages 28–37.

Verginica Barbu Mititelu and Elena Irimia. 2015. Types of errors in the automatic syntactic parsing of romanian. In *Errors by Humans and Machines in multimedia, multimodal and multilingual data processing. Proceedings of ERRARE 2015*. Sinaia, Romania, pages 195–204.

Cenel Augusto Perez. 2014. *Linguistic Resources for Natural Language Processing. (PhD thesis)*. Faculty of Computer Science, Al. I. Cuza University, Iași.

Petr Sgall, Eva Hajičová, and Jarmila Panevová. 1986. *The meaning of the sentence in its semantic and pragmatic aspects*. Academic Press and Reide, Prague, Dordrecht.

Kiril Simov and Petya Osenova. 2011. Towards minimal recursion semantics over bulgarian dependency parsing. In *Proceedings of the RANLP 2011 Conference*. Hissar, Bulgaria.

Zhiyi Song, Ann Bies, Stephanie Strassel, Tom Riese, Justin Mott, Joe Ellis, Jonathan Wright, Seth Kulick, Neville Ryant, and Xiaoyi Ma. 2015. From light to rich ere: Annotation of entities, relations, and events. In *Proceeding of 14th Annual Conference of the North American Chapter of the Association for Computational Linguistics*.

Pasi Tapanainen and Timo Jarvinen. 1998. Towards an implementable dependency grammar. In *CoLing-ACL98 workshop Processing of Dependency-based Grammars, Montreal*.

Lucien Tesnière. 1959. *Eléments de syntaxe structurale*. Klincksieck, Paris.

Diana Trandabăț. 2010. *Natural Language Processing Using Semantic Frames - PHD Thesis*. Faculty of Computer Science, Al. I. Cuza University, Iași.

Dan Tufiș, Verginica Barbu-Mititelu, Elena Irimia, Ștefan Dumitrescu, Tiberiu Boroș, Horia N. Teodorescu, Dan Cristea, Andrei Scutelnicu, Cecilia Bolea, Alex Moruz, and Laura Pistol. 1998. Corola starts blooming an update on the reference corpus of contemporary romanian language. In *Proceedings of the 3rd Workshop on Challenges in the Management of Large Corpora (CMLC-3)*.

GRaSP: Grounded Representation and Source Perspective

Antske Fokkens[♣], Piek Vossen[♣], Marco Rospocher[♢], Rinke Hoekstra[♡♣] and Willem R. van Hage[♠]
♣ CLTL and Computer Science, Vrije Universiteit, Amsterdam, The Netherlands
♢ Fondazione Bruno Kessler, Trento, Italy
♡ Elsevier BV, Amsterdam, The Netherlands
♠ Netherlands eScience Center, Amsterdam, The Netherlands
{antske.fokkens,piek.vossen}@vu.nl, rospocher@fbk.eu
r.hoekstra@elsevier.com, w.vanhage@esciencecenter.nl

Abstract

When people or organizations provide information, they make choices regarding **what** they include and **how** they represent it. These two aspects combined (the content and the stance) represent a **perspective**. Investigating perspectives can provide useful insights into the reliability of information, changes in viewpoints over time, shared beliefs among social or political groups and contrasts with other groups, etc. This paper introduces GRaSP, a generic framework for modeling perspectives and their sources.

1 Introduction

Structured data and knowledge resources typically provide what is seen as factual information. They contain definitions of concepts, ontologies, information about origins, dates, locations, etc. Methods have been developed to automatically extract such information from text (Hearst, 1992; Buitelaar et al., 2004; Wu and Weld, 2010, among others). However, knowledge consists of much more than ontological classifications and basic verifiable properties of objects and people. It involves information about various entities, events and concepts, connecting this information and judging its validity. For social science and humanities, these aspects of knowledge are particularly interesting, i.e. how information is connected, how people judge validity, how knowledge changes, what uncertainty and sentiment that accompanies it.

When people or organizations provide information, they make choices regarding what they include and how they present information. These two aspects together (the content and stance provided by the source) represent a *perspective*, an element of interest for many disciplines. Communication scientists and social psychologists study (e.g.) how common opinions or existing stereotypes are displayed in the media. Political scientists can investigate how various sources present hot topics. Historians may look into how perspectives on historic events change over time. Outside of academia, perspectives can be of interest to information professionals, decision makers, advertisers, journalists and any citizen interested in critical thinking and finding balanced information.

Natural language processing (NLP) can offer support in identifying the topic of text, classifying stances, identifying sentiment and opinions, determining factuality values of events, etc. To our knowledge, these technologies are generally investigated in isolation and have, up to date, not been connected in order to obtain a more full-fledged representation of perspectives. In this paper, we take the first step towards such a representation by introducing a framework that formally represents perspectives: the Grounded Representation and Source Perspective framework (GRaSP). GRaSP is a unique and generic flexible framework that combines the formal representation of the content and of the source perspective in one single model. It is compatible with existing models, but can also model subtleties that can be expressed in natural language but remain challenging for RDF representations.

The rest of this paper is structured as follows. We provide background on GRaSP in Section 2. We then introduce the framework itself in Section 3. We describe an automatically generated dataset represented in GRaSP in Section 4. After discussing related work, we conclude.

2 Background

The origins of GRaSP lie in the projects NewsReader (Vossen et al., 2016) and BiographyNet

Proceedings of Knowledge Resources for the Socio-Economic Sciences and Humanities associated with RANLP-17, pages 19–25,
Varna, Bulgaria, 7 Sep 2017.

(Fokkens et al., 2014). NewsReader aimed at extracting what happened to whom, when and where from large amounts of (financial) news, creating structured data to support decision making. In BiographyNet, we aimed to extract information about individuals in biographical dictionaries for historians. We investigated in connections between people and how the same person or event was depicted in different biographical dictionaries. An essential step for addressing these challenges is to indicate which documents talk about the same entity or event. In addition, the provenance of information is essential in both projects, i.e. end-users need insight into the source of specific information. NewsReader and BiographyNet also shared the vision of comparing differences in information from various sources.

More recent projects dive deeper in perspectives. *Understanding Language By Machines* investigates the relations between events, uncertainty, sentiment and opinons and how this information results into storylines and world views. In *Reading between the lines*, we look at more subtle cues of perspectives addressing questions such as "which background information given when talking about people from different ethnic groups?" or "when do we chose to generalize (e.g. by calling someone a thief rather than a suspect of having stolen something)?". QuPiD2 addresses (among others) what evidence is discussed and how sources build their argumentation around it.

With GRaSP, we aim to design a framework that can support the research questions central to these projects following six requirements. First, we want to represent various perspectives on the same entity, proposition or topic next to each other. Second, it should represent the source of each perspective, so that users can e.g. select all perspectives of a specific source; group sources according to shared or conflicting views on a given content; find all sources that have a perspective on the same content or share a perspective; and, find available background information about the source. Third, we want to provide the means to semantically compare the (propositional) content across statements and represent whether sources mention the same, similar or related content (e.g. more or less specific), or a different framing of content (e.g. *murdered*, which is intentional, or *killed* which may be accidental). Fourth, it should be possible to represent a wide range of perspective-related phenomena, including: sentiment, emotion, judgment, negation, certainty, speculation, reporting, framing and salience. Fifth, we want to make alternative *interpretations* of the same statement explicit, since statements might be (deliberately) ambiguous, not well formulated or difficult to process with Natural Language Processing (NLP) technology. Finally, users should be able to gain insight in the full provenance of any information provided by GRaSP. Next to the source, it should provide information about how this perspective was analyzed (e.g. expert analysis of a text, crowd annotations, text mining).

The first three requirements allow users to place various perspectives next to each other allowing them to compare, among others, which sources agree or disagree on what, which sources change their mind, which sources speculate and whether their predictions were accurate. In addition, they would allow identifying all content and stances given on a specific topic by a source and, for example, display this on a timeline. Researchers can thus investigate what information is important to sources who hold a specific opinion. The fourth and fifth requirement ensure that the model is flexible enough to support various needs of end-users as well as to accommodate the variation of information provided by different systems or datasets. Tools used to gather and interpret information can introduce biases end-users should be aware of (Lin, 2012; Rieder and Röhle, 2012). Providing clear provenance of information (including involved processes) is a necessary component for creating such awareness (sixth requirement).

There are several ontologies that can be used to model perspective-related information. We will outline the most influential ones and explain which part of the requirements they fulfill in Section 5.

3 The GRaSP Framework

Perspectives are expressed by **statements** (which can be spoken or written language, images, signals, etc.) from a specific source. A perspective can be conveyed in many ways, some more explicit than others. Explicit opinions or highly subjective terms are easily identified, but perspectives can be expressed more subtly. The selection and implicit framing of information plays a role (e.g. does an article report on someone's ethnicity, do they report an expert's political preference when citing them on a societal matter) as well as choices in how information is presented (e.g. using neutral or marked words, certainty, confirming or denying something). We therefore see a perspective as the combination of the **content** of one or more statements (which information is included) and the **stance** sources take on this content.

GRaSP makes the link between the content and stance of a statement as well as to their source explicit. The framework achieves this through a triple layered representation consisting of a **mention layer**, an **instance layer** and an **attribution layer**. The **mention layer** is the central layer of the model. Mentions are physical objects, such as a (piece of) text, (part of) an image or a sound, that signal information and can be embedded in a larger physical object. Mentions can be combined and form a statement that displays a perspective on some propositional content by some source. Propositions are abstract meaning representations that make reference to events and participating entities. Both events and entities are represented as instances in some (presumed) world in the **instance layer**. Finally, the stance expressed by the statement is represented in the **attribution layer**. This layer models attitudinal information such as beliefs, judgments, certainty and sentiment of the source towards the propositional content. This section introduces these layers and illustrate how they are used to model perspectives.[1]

3.1 Grounding

An essential part of representing perspectives is making explicit what the perspective is about, i.e. representing the described (real-world) situation. This is captured by the two top layers of our framework; the instance layer and the mention layer. These two layers, as well as their connecting relation are based on the architecture proposed in the Grounded Annotation Framework (Fokkens et al., 2013, GAF), which is incorporated in GRaSP. Consider the following examples:

1. During 2000-2014, measles vaccination prevent an estimated 17.1 million deaths

2. The search result contained 108 deaths over this period, resulting from four different measles vaccines

3. There have been no measles death reported in the U.S. since 2003

[1]The ontology and examples can be found at: https://github.com/cltl/GRaSP

These sentences above make statements about whether measles or vaccinations cause death. Figure 1 illustrates how this is represented in the top two layers of GRaSP.

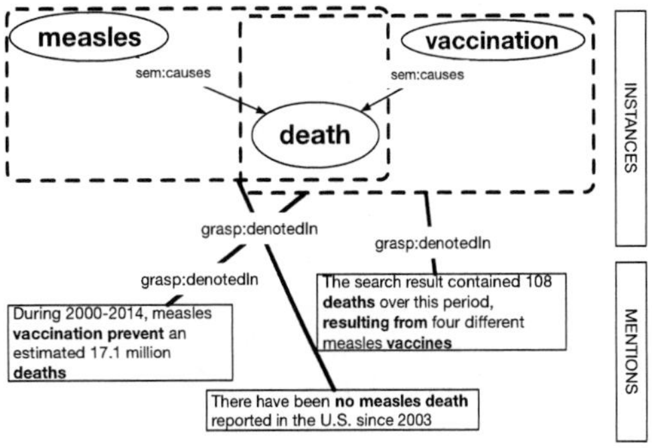

Figure 1: Instance and mention layers

The content of statements is represented in the instance layer. This layer can represent information about events, their participants, their locations or their time, but also information about (generic) concepts or ideas. Typically, propositions are expressed in terms of the Simple Event Model (SEM, (van Hage et al., 2011)), but information in this layer can be represented using other vocabularies as well. SEM is a generic RDF vocabulary for event-participant relations that allows for reasoning over the propositional content of statements. Event-event relations can be represented as well in the instance layer: the example in Figure 1 includes a causal relation between measles and death, and one between vaccination and death.

The second layer represents mentions. Mentions are (pieces of) resources that denote entities or propositions from the instance layer: they can be expressions in text, spoken words, numbers or signals on a display, images, videos, etc. The mention layer allows us to trace all resources where a specific event, a person or idea is mentioned. It also records each specific way in which an instance of interest is presented in a resource. Following Semantic Web practice, GRaSP identifies mentions by IRIs (Internationalized Resource Identifiers). This allows us to link them to additional information, including their surface string (the literal text) and lemma and their exact position within a text or image. This feature is particular relevant for scholars working with automatically analyzed text, since it allows them to easily identify where specific information is mentioned in the original source and hence verify it.

Entities, events and statements in the instance layer can be linked to expressions in the mention layer by the relations `grasp:denotedBy` pointing out the exact words or linguistic structure that expresses the event or statement, or by `grasp:denotedIn` which indicates that the statement is made somewhere in a sentence, paragraph or document. In our example the causal relation between 'vaccination' and 'death' is linked to Sentences 1. and 2. The relation between 'measles' and 'death' is linked to Sentence 3. Through these links, researchers interested in how various sources talk about the risks of measles or vaccinations can find snippets of text that talk about these issues. However, the source and the stance taken are not made explicit yet. The next subsection introduces the attribution layer, which allows us to add this information.

3.2 Source Perspective

Grounding (modeled by the link between instances and mentions) establishes what a specific message is about. Two components need to be added to complete a framework that can capture perspectives from various sources. First, mentions should be linked to the source that expresses the perspective. Second, we want to represent the stance the source takes on the content of the message. The stance typically includes information on factuality (e.g. does the source confirm or deny, is it certain or hesitant, is it talking about the future?), judgment, sentiment and emotion (e.g. does the source consider the content ethical, is the source scared by the content?).

The third layer, the **attribution** layer, adds these components to GRaSP. Figure 2 adds the attribution layer to our example. Each of the mentions is linked to an attribution node. These nodes are in turn linked to the source that published them and, if applicable, the source reported in the text. We use the PROV-DM (Moreau et al., 2013) to model the source of publication and a specified variant of the `wasAttributedTo` relation introduced by GRaSP for quoted sources. Attribution nodes also receive values that make the stance taken by the source explicit. In this case, the statements expressing opposing views to vaccines leading to deaths or measles leading to death are connected to a factuality value indicating that the source denied this relation without expressing doubt.

Through the addition of this layer, end-users can

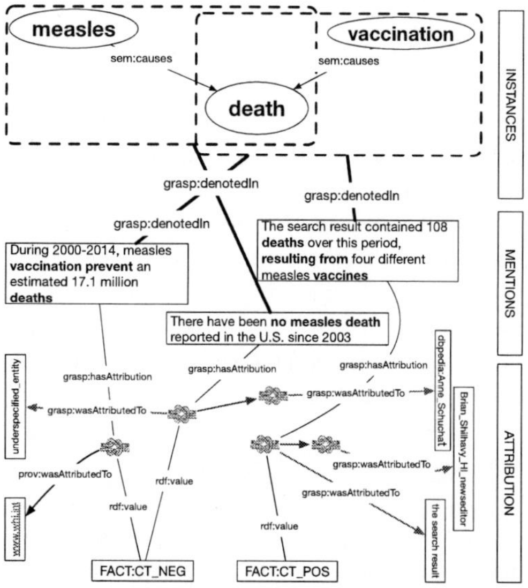

Figure 2: Instance, mention and attribution layers

explore opposing views on the same topic or statement. This allows users to compare sources reported on both viewpoints, identifying what other opinions these sources express and investigating the overall argumentation (the statement that there were no measles death can both been used by people opposing to vaccination, because "measles are not deadly", or by people supporting it, stating that "measles deaths are avoided thanks to vaccination"). Additional information about sources can be gathered leading to investigations on, among others, how reports on specific topics evaluate over time, the difference in certainty expressed by politicians or scientists or how different countries report on the same event.

The examples we have shown here are simplified for the purpose of illustration. Sentence 1. does not express the opposing view from vaccinations causes deaths by saying they do not, but exactly states vaccinations actively prevent death. This relation of prevention can also be modeled in GRaSP. Under this representation, we would model the statement that vaccination prevents death and that this forms an opposing view to them causing death. We can even model that both these statements can be considered to be true by the same source (e.g. believing that vaccinations avoid many deaths and sometimes cause them). The details of how to represent more complex relations and how viewpoints connect are beyond the scope of this paper.

4 GRaSP illustrated

One of the main challenges involved in representing perspectives in GRaSP is the question of how to obtain this information accurately. In principle, GRaSP can be used in combination with close-reading manual methods, where researchers use it to meticulously record the information they base their conclusions on. It becomes more interesting when we can represent massive amounts of data and help researchers find information automatically. Sentiment analysis, factuality classification, opinion mining, event extraction and argumentation mining are challenging tasks. Automatically creating highly accurate representations of perspectives in GRaSP is a challenge for the future. Nevertheless, current methods can provide output that we believe to be useful for researchers interested in perspectives. In this section, we illustrate what information can currently be generated by NLP tools through a dataset that the GRaSP framework for representation made available through an interface providing an open source visualization (van der Zwaan et al., 2016; van Meersbergen et al., 2017).

The GRaSP dataset consists of WikiNews texts[2] by the Open Source pipeline of NewsReader (Vossen et al., 2016). The pipeline includes software for identifying events, relations between events, factuality of events and opinions. The interpretation program turning the linguistic representations of the NLP tools into RDF representation in GRaSP specifically targets Source Introducing Predicates (e.g. *say*, *believe*), identifying who said what according to the text. All content not in the scope of these predicates is attributed to the author of the text.

The interactive visualization showing perspectives on immigration and external EU borders in WikiNews.[3] is available on github and can be explored for better understanding of the following passage.[4] Figure 3 provides a partial screenshot. On the left hand side, the sources are provided. There are two lists of sources, the bottom list provides the authors or publishers of news articles. The top list provides sources quoted in the article. The events mentioned by the sources are displayed in the central image, with actual text on the right. Statistics on sentiment and factuality are provided by the diagrams at the bottom of the visualization. The visualization is interactive: sources and events can be selected leading to updates of perspective information and text.

5 Related Work

GRaSP offers ways to connect statements (in texts, video, images, etc.) to their source, the entities and events they mention and the stance they display. Arguably, this connection can be seen as a form of *annotation*. The Web Annotation Data Model (OA)[5] of the W3C represents annotations as the *related* combination of a body (the annotation) and a target (the annotated source). The relation is *directed*, the body says something about the target, but not vice versa. Directionality of OA, and the annotation view in general, is not compatible with the goals of GRaSP. A traditional annotation would just say that the link between an instance and its mention is a form of semantic enrichment of the text containing mention. The real question is: does the semantic representation of an instance determine how mentions should be understood, or do the combined mentions of an instance collectively determine its semantics? This nuance is of central importance when e.g. studying concept drift across historical sources, and it is the reason that GRaSP commits to the neutral *denotation* relation between instances and mentions. Secondly, the OA specification forces annotation targets to be *dereferencable*, which is problematic for sources that are not owned by the agent producing the annotations. License and other constraints may prohibit republication, and on a technical level dereferenceability cannot be guaranteed for sources hosted at an external location.

Marl[6] provides a model to represent subjective opinions in text. Marl is used by the Onyx ontology[7] for representing emotions expressed in text. It has also been combined with lexical information on sentiment from Lemon (Buitelaar et al., 2013).[8] GRaSP shares this flexibility of being compatible with various models that express aspects of perspectives. Unlike GRaSP, Marl is restricted to text. It furthermore confounds the layers that GRaSP carefully separates: the opinion (attribution in GRaSP) is a central node, that refers to

[2]https://en.wikinews.org/wiki/Main_Page

[3]http://wikinews.org/

[4]http://nlesc.github.io/UncertaintyVisualization/

[5]http://www.w3.org/TR/annotation-model/

[6]http://gsi.dit.upm.es/ontologies/marl/

[7]http://www.gsi.dit.upm.es/ontologies/onyx/

[8]http://lemon-model.net

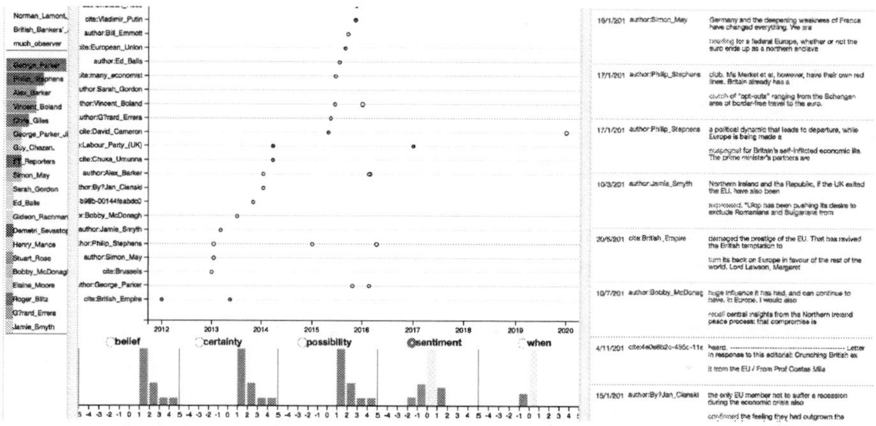

Figure 3: Screenshot of visualized perspective information

an object/feature (instance in GRaSP) and the literal text that reflects the opinion (mentions). This has two consequences. First, Marl only relates the opinion to the source (text or url) in which it was found without making the opinion holder explicit. GRaSP links mentions to their provenance and attributions of stances to the source that expressed the opinion. Marl thus does not seem to provide the means to collect all perspectives from a specific source. Second, GRaSP's separation of these layers makes it more flexible in dealing with alternative interpretations of mentions, both at the attribution and instance layer. Finally, GRaSP is not limited to explicitly subjective opinions, but can connect all stances taken by a source (including factual statements).

GRaSP can be combined with various existing models. We use PROV (Moreau et al., 2013) to model the provenance of mentions and interpretations made on them (i.e. to model the NLP process following Ockeloen et al. (2013)). The NLP Interchange Format (NIF, Hellmann et al. 2013) is an RDF/OWL vocabulary for representing NLP annotations in a common way, to foster interoperability between NLP tools, language resources and annotations. The core of NIF consists of a vocabulary and a URI design that permit describing strings and substrings, to which arbitrary annotations can be attached using vocabularies external to NIF. NIF itself does not specifically address the representation of source or attribution information, but can be combined with GRaSP. GRaSP bases the format of IRIs of mentions on NIF and uses it to represent some mention layer attributes (e.g. char offset in the text). Finally, GRaSP uses the grounding relations provided by GAF, as mentioned above. GRaSP's main contribution compared to GAF is that GRaSP adds an attribution layer tying sources and their stances to mentions.

6 Conclusion and Discussion

This paper introduces GRaSP, a formal framework to represent perspectives on content. The GRaSP framework was designed out of need from various NLP projects that deal with automatically identifying perspectives. We explained how GRaSP provides the structure to study perspectives from various view points (starting with a topic, source, sentiment, or stance). We provide a dataset actively using GRaSP that allows users to study the perspective various sources express on events in WikiNews.

The way perspectives are expressed in natural language is highly complex. Space limitations prevented us to illustrate how phenomena such as scope, alternative interpretations and framing can be represented in GRaSP. The wide range of possibilities for applying this and how researchers can deal with (lack of) accuracy of NLP tools also requires more space than available in a short paper. We plan to address these issues in future work.

Acknowledgement

The work presented in this paper was funded by the European Union through the FP7 project NewsReader and by the Netherlands Organization for Scientific Research (NWO) via the Spinoza grant, awarded to Piek Vossen and via VENI grant 275-89-029 awarded to Antske Fokkens.

References

Paul Buitelaar, Mihael Arcan, Carlos A Iglesias, J Fernando Sánchez-Rada, and Carlo Strapparava. 2013. Linguistic linked data for sentiment analysis. In *2nd Workshop on Linked Data in Linguistics*. page 1.

Paul Buitelaar, Daniel Olejnik, and Michael Sintek. 2004. A protégé plug-in for ontology extraction from text based on linguistic analysis. In *European Semantic Web Symposium*. Springer, pages 31–44.

Antske Fokkens, Serge Ter Braake, Niels Ockeloen, Piek Vossen, Susan Legêne, and Guus Schreiber. 2014. Biographynet: Methodological issues when nlp supports historical research. In *LREC*. pages 3728–3735.

Antske Fokkens, Marieke van Erp, Piek Vossen, Sara Tonelli, Willem Robert van Hage, Luciano Serafini, Rachele Sprugnoli, and Jesper Hoeksema. 2013. GAF: A grounded annotation framework for events. In *The 1st Workshop on Events*. Atlanta, USA.

Marti A Hearst. 1992. Automatic acquisition of hyponyms from large text corpora. In *Proceedings of the 14th conference on Computational linguistics-Volume 2*. Association for Computational Linguistics, pages 539–545.

Sebastian Hellmann, Jens Lehmann, Sren Auer, and Martin Brmmer. 2013. Integrating NLP using Linked Data. In *Proc. of ISWC*. pages 98–113. See also `http://persistence.uni-leipzig.org/nlp2rdf/`.

Yu-wei Lin. 2012. Transdisciplinarity and digital humanities: Lessons learned from developing text-mining tools for textual analysis. In *Understanding digital humanities*, Springer, pages 295–314.

Luc Moreau, Paolo Missier, Khalid Belhajjame, Reza B'Far, James Cheney, Sam Coppens, Stephen Cresswell, Yolanda Gil, Paul Groth, Graham Klyne, et al. 2013. Prov-dm: The prov data model. *Retrieved July* 30:2013.

Niels Ockeloen, Antske Fokkens, Serge Ter Braake, Piek Vossen, Victor De Boer, Guus Schreiber, and Susan Legêne. 2013. Biographynet: Managing provenance at multiple levels and from different perspectives. In *LiSc-Volume 1116*. CEUR-WS. org, pages 59–71.

Bernhard Rieder and Theo Röhle. 2012. Digital methods: Five challenges. In *Understanding digital humanities*, Springer, pages 67–84.

Janneke van der Zwaan, Maarten van Meersbergen, Antske Fokkens, Serge ter Braake, Inger Leemans, Erika Kuijpers, Piek Vossen, and Isa Maks. 2016. Storyteller: Visualizing perspectives in digital humanities projects. In *Computational History and Data-Driven Humanities: Second IFIP WG 12.7 International Workshop, CHDDH 2016, Dublin, Ireland, May 25, 2016, Revised Selected Papers 2*. Springer, pages 78–90.

Willem Robert van Hage, Véronique Malaisé, Roxane Segers, Laura Hollink, and Guus Schreiber. 2011. Design and use of the Simple Event Model (SEM). *Journal of Web Semantics* 9(2):128–136.

Maarten van Meersbergen, Piek Vossen, Janneke van der Zwaan, Antske Fokkens, Willem van Hage, Inger Leemans, and Isa Maks. 2017. Storyteller: Visual analytics of perspectives on rich text interpretations. In *Proceedings of Natural Language Processing meets Journalism*. Copenhagen, Denmark.

Piek Vossen, Rodrigo Agerri, Itziar Aldabe, Agata Cybulska, Marieke van Erp, Antske Fokkens, Egoitz Laparra, Anne-Lyse Minard, Alessio Palmero Aprosio, German Rigau, Marco Rospocher, and Roxane Segers. 2016. Newsreader: Using knowledge resources in a cross-lingual reading machine to generate more knowledge from massive streams of news. *Knowledge-Based Systems* 110:60–85.

Fei Wu and Daniel S Weld. 2010. Open information extraction using wikipedia. In *Proceedings of the 48th Annual Meeting of the Association for Computational Linguistics*. Association for Computational Linguistics, pages 118–127.

Educational Content Generation for Business and Administration FL Courses with the NBU PLT Platform

Associate Prof. Dr. Maria STAMBOLIEVA
Laboratory for Language Technologies, New Bulgarian University
mstambolieva@nbu.bg

Abstract

The paper presents a project of the Laboratory for Language Technologies of New Bulgarian University (NBU) – "E-Platform for Language Teaching (PLT)[1]" – the development of corpus-based teaching content for Business English courses. The following methodological issues are briefly discussed to present the background for the development of the platform: 1. problems of e-learning; 2. problems of communicative foreign language teaching; 3. problems of teaching foreign languages for specific purposes; 4. E-learning at NBU. The structure and functionalities of the platform are then outlined, with a focus on corpus development and test generation in teaching foreign languages for specific purposes (TFLSP).

1 E-learning

E-learning is an important part of modern foreign language acquisition. The Internet abounds in freely accessible language tests, graded presentations of thematic vocabulary and grammar. It also offers freely accessible authentic texts, audio and visual information – which can be used for the purpose of language learning. Most often used as a supplement to traditional classroom tuition, e-learning can be an invaluable means of increasing the overall effectiveness of the process of teaching– especially if sufficiently well planned and conceived as an integral part of this process.

The integration of digital instruction with the traditional educational context – known as "blended learning", has been gaining ground since the early years of the new millennium. Bonk and Graham2 define it as the combination of "face-to-face instruction with computer mediated instruction". The technological equipment and know-how of teachers and students now being more or less taken for granted, blended learning takes advantage of the versatility of the Internet as a medium of communication. While providing opportunities for personalisation of educational content and individualisation in timing and pace, effective blended learning requires no less careful planning and preparation than traditional brick-and-mortar classes; and the simple addition of available online videos or tests to existing educational content might lend a course flavor but will not necessarily increase its effectiveness.

The need to plan and organise teaching material has resulted in the development of educational platforms. Platforms with ready-for-use content are offered by many publishing houses specialising in foreign language teaching aids and are very popular in schools; most universities however make use of their own platforms, where lecturers develop their own courses. The PLT educational content can be integrated in both.

[1] Project funded by the Central Fund for the Strategic Development of NBU for the period 2016-2017.

[2] Bonk, C.J. & Graham, C.R. *(2006). The handbook of blended learning environments: Global perspectives, local designs.* San Francisco: Jossey-Bass/Pfeiffer. p. 5.

Proceedings of Knowledge Resources for the Socio-Economic Sciences and Humanities associated with RANLP-17, pages 26–30, Varna, Bulgaria, 7 Sep 2017.

Figure 1. Structure of the platform: modules

2 E-learning at NBU

New Bulgarian University is unique not only in Bulgaria, but also in the area of Central and Eastern Europe in that 1/ it offers its students over 120 hours per semester of compulsory foreign language teaching and 2/ it makes extensive (again, compulsory) use of the Moodle educational platform.

While Moodle is compulsory, not all of its functionalities are made use of by all lecturers. Some simply post additional reading, homework or short messages to the group, others use the forum for group discussions. The necessity to make fuller use of the platform in foreign language classes arose from a recent survey showing a drop in student attendance and performance. Accordingly, the year 2016 marked the development of: 1/ a unified "backbone" educational content for blended or distance learning for each CEFRL; 2/ the development of the PLT as an additional support to Moodle-based general language courses and a main support to courses in foreign languages for specific purposes. One of the major aims of the PLT project is to provide course support for lecturers and students in the over 50 BA programs of the university in the form of domain-specific online texts, text-based exercises and tests for both regular and distance-learning programmes and courses.

3 Teaching FL for specific purposes

Following several successful pilot tests during the academic year 2016/2017, from October 2017 weekly PLT-based tuition will be available for students taking courses in the "Applied Foreign Languages for Administration and Management" BA programme. In designing the course, we have followed McDonough and J.S. Shaw (1993: 243ff.) who define the ideal system for teaching foreign languages for specific purposes as one that allows individualisation of the learning process. In the usual conditions (classroom, group) such individualisation can hardly be achieved: while the needs of the trainees are symmetrical, the groups are often heterogeneous – which can significantly reduce the motivation of the learners. As P. Hemingway (1987: 18) points out,

> "a mixed level class can be demotivating for students if they are not encouraged to work to their own limits, and enabled to fully participate in the lesson. The student whose English is more advanced than the rest may feel cut off from the group if he/she is constantly given work to do alone, while the others catch up".

Foreign language teaching for specific purposes does not necessarily follow training in the general-purpose language; it can successfully be conducted alongside with it, or even on its own (Cf. Dudley-Evans & St. John, 1998: 4-5). It should provide the trainees with the freedom to choose the learning content and provide them with appropriate teaching material and sufficient training exercises. The learning process has a greater degree of autonomy and greater freedom of choice as to when, what, and how to study. The role of the lecturer is reduced to that of a professional consultant who designs the course, selects (possibly adapts) the teaching materials, designs and arranges the exercises to them, checks and evaluates the work of the students. (Cf. Carver 1989: 134).

4 Structure and functionalities of the Platform

The PLT system comprises:

- a repository of domain-specific texts, further classified in accordance with the Common European Framework of Reference for Languages (CEFRL);
- a module for corpus creation;
- a linguistic data base integrating the results of lemmatisation, POS-tagging, morphemic and syntactic analysis, term identification and definition, multiple-word term identification;
- a set of test-generation modules generating drills based on: a. text degradation, b. reordering, c. multiple matching;
- a concordance and a parallel texts aligner.

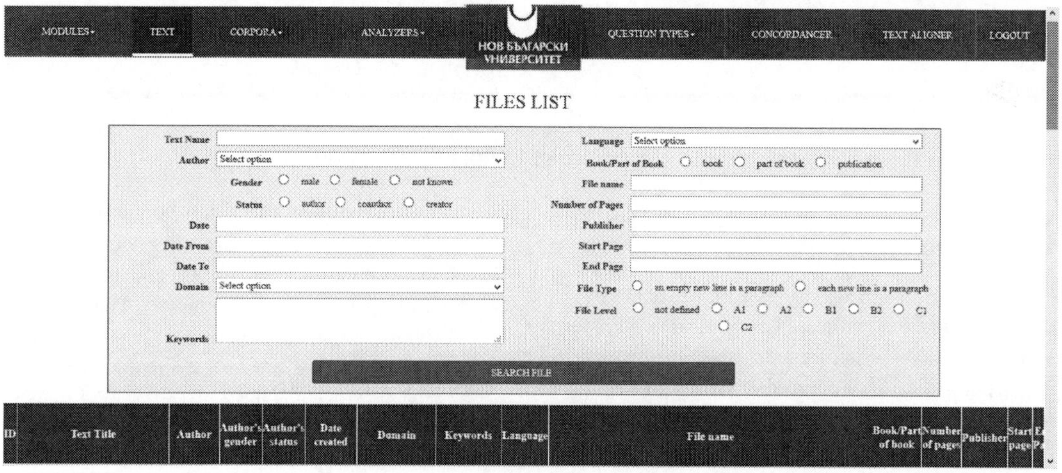

Figure 2. The PLT text classifier

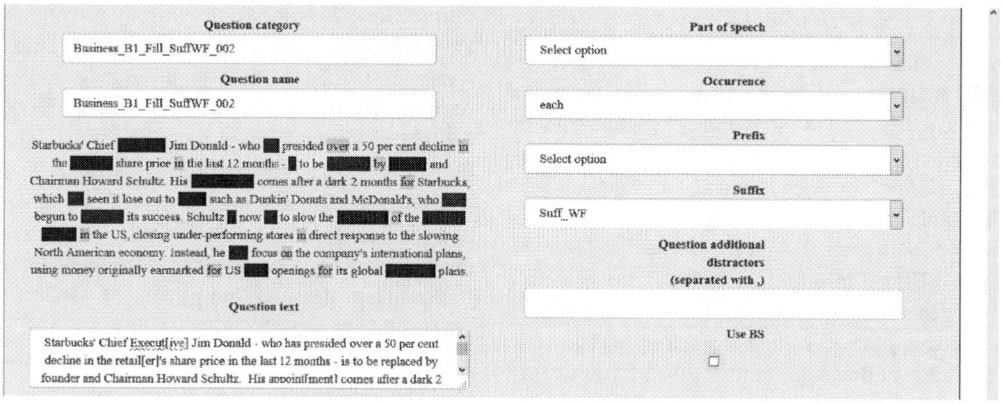

Figure 3. Generation of a Fill in the Blanks exercise in the PLT

5 Creating a Domain- and CEFRL-based corpus

The corpus for the domain of Administration and Business is, for now, subdivided into four sub-corpora – for the CEFRL levels A1, A2, B1 and B2 (to be extended shortly to C1 and C2). Most texts have been selected from freely accessible sites for business, business news and business writing. In assessing difficulty levels, Laurence Anthony's AntWordProfiler[3] is used alongside with personal expertise.

The corpora can be united to form general domain-based or other text profile-based corpora; they can also be split. New corpora can be created by corpus-merging operations or by document selection.

6 Task Generation and the Language Task Bank

The platform allows the creation of a variety of language drills of the following main types:

- **Text degradation** exercises based on lemmtisation (open the brackets using an appropriate word form), POS tagging (e.g. fill in the blanks with an appropriate noun / verb / adjective article / preposition, etc.), morphemic analysis (e.g. select/type in an appropriate prefix/ suffix / root). The format of the exercises can be Drag-and-drop, Drop-down or Fill in (Open cloze).
- **Multiple matching** of terms with definitions, synonyms, information from encyclo-

[3] http://www.laurenceanthony.net/software/antwordprofiler/releases/AntWordProfiler141/help.pdf

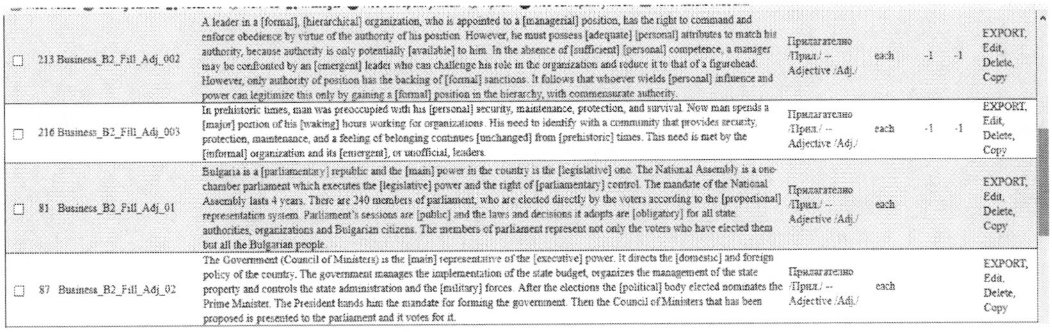

☐	213 Business_B2_Fill_Adj_002	A leader in a [formal], [hierarchical] organization, who is appointed to a [managerial] position, has the right to command and enforce obedience by virtue of the authority of his position. However, he must possess [adequate] [personal] attributes to match his authority, because authority is only potentially [available] to him. In the absence of [sufficient] [personal] competence, a manager may be confronted by an [emergent] leader who can challenge his role in the organization and reduce it to that of a figurehead. However, only authority of position has the backing of [formal] sanctions. It follows that whoever wields [personal] influence and power can legitimize this only by gaining a [formal] position in the hierarchy, with commensurate authority.	Прилагателно /Прил./ -- Adjective /Adj./	each	-1	-1	EXPORT, Edit, Delete, Copy
☐	216 Business_B2_Fill_Adj_003	In prehistoric times, man was preoccupied with his [personal] security, maintenance, protection, and survival. Now man spends a [major] portion of his [waking] hours working for organizations. His need to identify with a community that provides security, protection, maintenance, and a feeling of belonging continues [unchanged] from [prehistoric] times. This need is met by the [informal] organization and its [emergent], or unofficial, leaders.	Прилагателно /Прил./ -- Adjective /Adj./	each	-1	-1	EXPORT, Edit, Delete, Copy
☐	81 Business_B2_Fill_Adj_01	Bulgaria is a [parliamentary] republic and the [main] power in the country is the [legislative] one. The National Assembly is a one-chamber parliament which executes the [legislative] power and the right of [parliamentary] control. The mandate of the National Assembly lasts 4 years. There are 240 members of parliament, who are elected directly by the voters according to the [proportional] representation system. Parliament's sessions are [public] and the laws and decisions it adopts are [obligatory] for all state authorities, organizations and Bulgarian citizens. The members of parliament represent not only the voters who have elected them but all the Bulgarian people.	Прилагателно /Прил./ -- Adjective /Adj./	each			EXPORT, Edit, Delete, Copy
☐	87 Business_B2_Fill_Adj_02	The Government (Council of Ministers) is the [main] representative of the [executive] power. It directs the [domestic] and foreign policy of the country. The government manages the implementation of the state budget, organizes the management of the state property and controls the state administration and the [military] forces. After the elections the [political] body elected nominates the Prime Minister. The President hands him the mandate for forming the government. Then the Council of Ministers that has been proposed is presented to the parliament and it votes for it.	Прилагателно /Прил./ -- Adjective /Adj./	each			EXPORT, Edit, Delete, Copy

Figure 4. Exercises generated on the platform

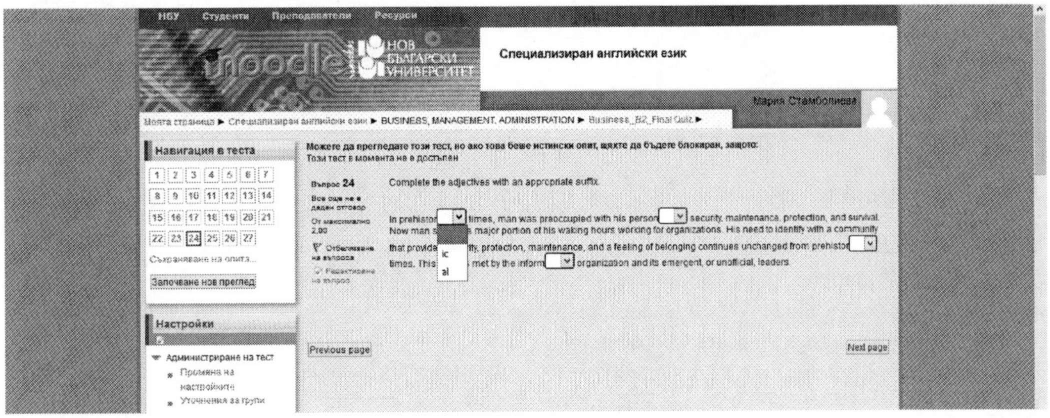

Figure 5. Text-based test

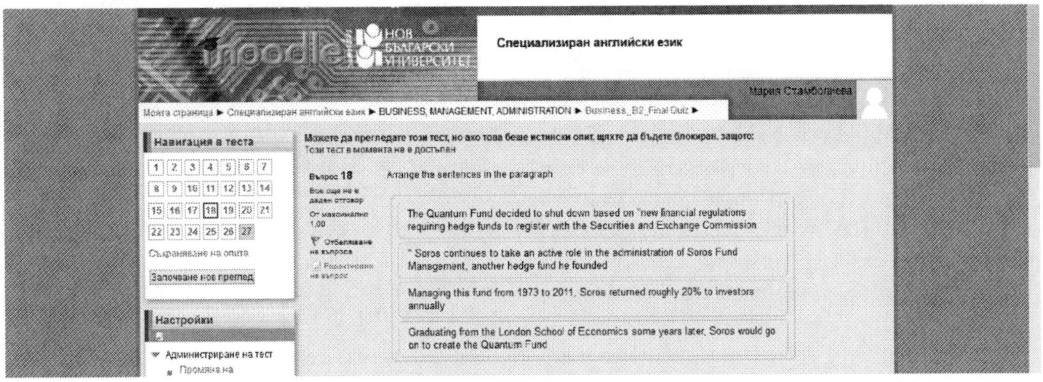

Figure 6. Rearranging task (sentences in paragraph)

pedia, translations – whatever has been entered in the definition box for the term marked at the bottom of the POS analyser. While the methodology of communicative language teaching (CLT) excludes translation, establishing translation equivalence in terminology is an important element of TFLSP – hence the option for translation equivalents of terms in the data base, plus the recent addition of a parallel texts aligner to the system (integration: in development).

- **Reordering drills**. The platform allows reordering drills for words, phrases and clauses in sentence, sentences in paragraphs and paragraphs in text. Exercises can be edited, if necessary, both in the task-generation module and in the task bank.

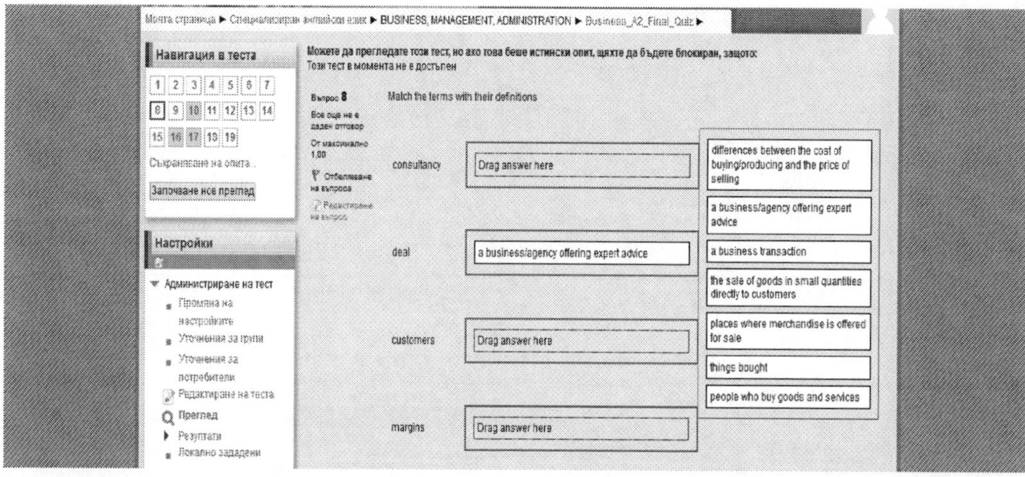

Figure 7. Terminology: Multiple choice 1

7 Test generation

The exercises are exported from the platform to a directory and, from there, imported into the educational platform used by the university, school, institute, publishing house, etc. In Moodle, they can be grouped in different ways in tests designed by the tutor. These tests can be either based on one or more texts (and include a variety of lexical or grammatical exercises), or else on task types (e.g. multiple matching exercises for terminology, Fill in the blanks exercises for articles, etc.).

Figure 6 above is a screenshot of a text-based test with 27 different tasks, where task 24 is a multiple choice drop-down exercise on word formation. Task 18 in Figure 6 is a reordering exercise. The task in Figure 7 is a multiple choice exercise on terminology. The order in which the tasks appear in the test can be fixed or variable. Tests can be repeated a limited or unlimited number of times.

8 Concluding remarks

The NBU E-platform for language teaching is a flexible, versatile tool which can be used for both education and research. In its application to foreign language teaching for specific purposes, it can successfully support the development of blended or distant courses, offering most of the advantages of e-learning over bricks-and-mortar classes: abundance of drilling material with special attention to structure/form and accuracy, individualisation and personalisation of the learning process, attention to the learner's native language and to accuracy of translation, development of self-reliance and motivation, immediate student and tutor feedback and easy centralized monitoring.

After less than a year of successful testing, the PLT is gradually becoming part and parcel of the general and specialised language teaching at NBU. The creation and constant development of the CEFRL corpus in the domain of business and administration allows the introduction of PLT-based tuition from the academic year 2017/2018.

References

Anthony, Laurence 2014. http://www.laurence-anthony.net/software/antwordprofiler/releases/AntWordProfiler141/help.pdf

Bonk, C.J. & Graham, C.R. (2006). *The handbook of blended learning environments: Global perspectives, local designs*. San Francisco: Jossey-Bass/Pfeiffer. p. 5.

Carver, D. 1983. *Some propositions about ESP.* The ESP Journal, 2, pp. 131-137.

Dudley-Evans, T, M. St John, 1998. *Developments in ESP: A multi-disciplinary approach.* Cambridge: Cambridge University Press.

Hemingway, P., 1986. *Teaching a mixed-level class*, Practical English Teaching, pp. 18-20.

McDonough, J., C. 1993. Shaw. *Materials and Methods in ELT*. Cambridge, Mass.: Blackwell.

Machine Learning Models of Universal Grammar Parameter Dependencies

Dimitar Kazakov
Dept. of Comp. Science
University of York
dlk2@york.ac.uk

Guido Cordoni
Dept. of Lang. and Ling. Sci.
University of York
gc927@york.ac.uk

Andrea Ceolin
Dept. of Linguistics
U. of Pennsylvania
ceolin@sas.upenn.edu

Monica A. Irimia
Dept. of Comm. and Econ.
U. of Modena and Reggio Emilia
irimiamo@unimore.it

Shin-Sook Kim
Dept. of Lang. and Ling. Sci
University of York
sk899@york.ac.uk

Dimitris Michelioudakis
Dept. of Lang. and Ling. Sci.
University of York
dm9540@york.ac.uk

Nina Radkevich
Dept. of Lang. and Ling. Sci.
University of York
nr6920@york.ac.uk

Cristina Guardiano
Dip. Com. ed Econ.
UniMORE
cguardiano@unimore.it

Giuseppe Longobardi
Dept. of Lang. and Ling. Sci.
University of York
gl6730@york.ac.uk

Abstract

The use of parameters in the description of natural language syntax has to balance between the need to discriminate among (sometimes subtly different) languages, which can be seen as a cross-linguistic version of Chomsky's (1964) descriptive adequacy, and the complexity of the acquisition task that a large number of parameters would imply, which is a problem for explanatory adequacy. Here we present a novel approach in which a machine learning algorithm is used to find dependencies in a table of parameters. The result is a dependency graph in which some of the parameters can be fully predicted from others. These empirical findings can be then subjected to linguistic analysis, which may either refute them by providing typological counter-examples of languages not included in the original dataset, dismiss them on theoretical grounds, or uphold them as tentative empirical laws worth of further study.

1 Introduction

Parametric theories of generative grammar focus on the problem of a formal and principled theory of grammatical diversity (Chomsky, 1981; Baker, 2001; Roberts, 2012). The basic intuition of parametric approaches is that the majority of observable syntactic differences among languages are derived, usually through complex deductive chains, from a smaller number of more abstract contrasts, drawn from a universal list of discrete, and normally binary, options, called parameters. The relation between observable patterns and the actual syntactic parameters which vary across languages is quite indirect: syntactic parameters are regarded as abstract differences often responsible for wider typological clusters of surface co-variation, often through an intricate deductive structure. In this sense, the concept of parametric data is not to be simplistically identified with that of syntactic pattern: co-varying syntactic properties/patterns are in fact the empirical manifestations of much more abstract cognitive structures.

Syntactic parameters are conceived as definable by UG (i.e. universally comparable) and set by each learner on the basis of her/his linguistic environment. Open parameters, or any set of more primitive concepts they can derive from (Longobardi, 2005; Lightfoot, 2017), define a variation space for biologically acquirable grammars, set (a.k.a. *closed*) parameters specify each of these grammars. Thus, the core grammar of every natural language can in principle be represented by a string of binary symbols (Clark and Roberts, 1993), each coding the value of a parameter of UG.

The Parametric Comparison Method (PCM, (Longobardi and Guardiano, 2009)) uses syntactic parameters to study historical

Proceedings of Knowledge Resources for the Socio-Economic Sciences and Humanities associated with RANLP-17, pages 31–37,
Varna, Bulgaria, 7 Sep 2017.

relationships among languages. An important aspect of parametric systems that is particularly relevant to the present research is that parameters form a pervasive network of partial implications (Guardiano and Longobardi, 2005; Longobardi and Guardiano, 2009; Longobardi et al., 2013): one particular value of some parameter A, but not the other, often entails the irrelevance of parameter B, whose consequences, i.e. the corresponding surface patterns, become predictable. Under such conditions, B becomes redundant and will not be set at all by the learner. The PCM system makes such interdependencies explicit: in our notation, he symbols + and − are used to represent the binary value of each parameter; the symbol '0', instead, encodes the neutralising effect of implicational cross-parametric dependencies, i.e. cases in which the content of a parameter is either entirely predictable, or irrelevant altogether. The conditions which must hold for each parameter not to be neutralised are expressed in a Boolean form, i.e., either as simple states of another parameter (or negation thereof), or as conjunctions or disjunctions of values of other parameters.

The PCM has shown that an important effect of the pervasiveness of parameter interdependencies is a noticeable downsizing of the space of grammatical variation: according to some preliminary experiments (Bortolussi et al., 2011), the number of possible languages generated from a given set of independent binary parameters is reduced from 10^{18} to 10^{11} when their interdependencies are taken into account. This also crucially implies a noticeable reduction of the space of possible languages that a learner has to navigate when acquiring a language.

Here we adopt an empirical, data-driven approach to the task of identifying parameter dependencies, which has been implemented on a database of 71 languages described through the values of 91 syntactic parameters (see Appendix A) expressing the internal syntax of nominal structures. Our results show that applying machine learning techniques to the data reveals previously unknown dependencies between parameters, which could potentially lead to a further significant reduction of the search space of possible languages.

if $P_1 = +$ **and** $P_2 = -$ **then**
  $P_3 = +$
else
  $P_3 = -$

Figure 1: Parameter dependency model example

This paper sets out to identify parameters whose entire range of values can be fully predicted from the values of other parameters. There is an important difference between previously published work on parameter dependencies and this paper's contribution, which needs to be emphasised: rather than state that, for example, any language in which $P_1 =$ + will have a fully predictable value of P_2 (a fact which we encode as $P_2 = 0$), we seek parameters whose value can be deduced in *all* cases from the values of certain other parameters, e.g. as shown in the hypothetical example in Figure 1. Should such a rule prove to have universal validity, then parameter P_3 would never offer any advantage in separating any two languages, yet it could clearly still play a useful role in describing them.

2 Learning Dependencies

We process our table of dimensions ($\#lang \times \#param$) with the data mining package WEKA (*v*.3.6.13) (Hall et al., 2009). More specifically, we take the values of all parameters but one for all languages (i.e. a dataset of size ($\#lang \times \#param - 1$), and learn a decision tree that predicts the value of the remaining parameter from the values of the other parameters. (Typically, only a few are necessary in each case.) This is repeated to produce a decision tree for each of the parameters. The machine learning algorithm used was ID3 (Quinlan, 1986). The algorithm produces a decision tree, in which each leaf corresponds to the value of the modelled parameter for the combination of parameter values listed on the way from the root to that leaf, e.g.: **if** $FGN = -$ **and** $FGP = +$ **then** $GCO = +$ (see Table 1). Unlike some of the more sophisticated decision tree learning algorithms, such as C4.5 (Quinlan, 1993), no postprocessing of the tree learnt (such as *pruning* (Mitchell, 1997)) takes place, and the tree remains an accurate, exact reflection of the training data. If the combination of parameter values corresponding to one of the leaves of the tree is not observed in the data, the leaf contains the special label 'null' (see the tree predicting *GCO* in Table 1). In all other cases, that is, whenever the leaf label is '+', '-' or '0', this is supported by one or more examples (languages) in the data.

Table 1: Examples of decision trees for parameters FGN and GCO

```
~~~~~~~~~~~~~~~~~~
FGN:
if GCO = 0 then FGN = +
if GCO = + then FGN = -
if GCO = - then FGN = -
~~~~~~~~~~~~~~~~~~
GCO:
if FGN = 0 then GCO = null    ;never occurs
if FGN = + then GCO = 0
if FGN = - then
   if FGP = 0 then GCO = null;never occurs
   if FGP = + then GCO = +
   if FGP = - then GCO = -
~~~~~~~~~~~~~~~~~~
```

3 Results

The decision trees for all parameters were used to produce a dependency graph in which each vertex represents a parameter, and directed edges link the parameters, whose values are needed to predict a given parameter, with the node representing that parameter. For instance, there are edges from both *FGN* and *FGP* to *GCO*, as the decision tree for *GCO* refers to the values of *FGN* and *FGP*. Some of the decision trees are more complex, making use of up to nine separate parameters. The resulting graph is very complex (see Fig. 2).Therefore, we also present a subset of the graph (see Fig. 3), which only visualises those trees predicting one parameter from the value of one (as in the case of *FGN*) or two other parameters (e.g. *GCO*). The fact that some of the rules are missing from this graph is not an issue: for each listed node, all of the incoming edges are present, so that if we know those parameters, we are guaranteed to know the parameter they point to.

The interpretation of the graph is straightforward. For instance, looking at its top right corner, one can deduce that for any language in the dataset, it is enough to know the values of parameters $EZ3$ and PLS in order to know the value of $EZ2$, and therefore, of $EZ1$, too. Knowing (the value of) FVP means one also knows DMG and NSD; if one knows both FVP and DNN, the values of DNG, NSD, DSN, DMP and DMG are fully predictable for the given data set. In other words, 7 parameters (FVP, DNN, DNG, NSD, DSN, DMP and DMG) can be reduced to just 2 without any loss of information.

Some of the rules identified by the algorithm are not new, and are already contained in the dataset, as encoded by the implicational system described in Section 1. For instance, the parameter RHM is encoded as 0 when $FGP = -$, as the value of RHM is fully predictable in those cases. When a decision tree predicting FGP is learned, the result is as follows: **if** $RHM = 0$ **then** $FGP = -$ **else** $FGP = +$.

Even the rest of the rules learned are still just empirical findings that may change with the addition of other examples of languages or their validity may be questioned by linguists on theoretical grounds.

Linguistic analysis of the results is ongoing, and while no part of the results has been accepted as sufficient evidence to dispose of a parameter, implication rules may be revised on the basis of the decision trees learned, as in the case of the parameter PLS. According to its definition, the parameter "*asks if in a language without grammaticalized Number, a plural marker can also appear outside a nominal phrase, marking a distributive relation between the plural subject and the constituent bearing it.*" (E.g. $PLS = +$ for Korean, but $PLS = -$ for Japanese.)

Prior to this research, there was an implication rule stating that PLS is neutralised (that is, its value is predictable) for all combinations of CGO and FGN values other than $CGO = -$ and $FGN = -$. This rule has now been replaced with a new rule stating that PLS is neutralised for all combinations of values of FGM and FGN, except when $FGM = +$ and $FGN = -$, and the evidence showing that the new rule is consistent with the data came from the tree learned for PLS.

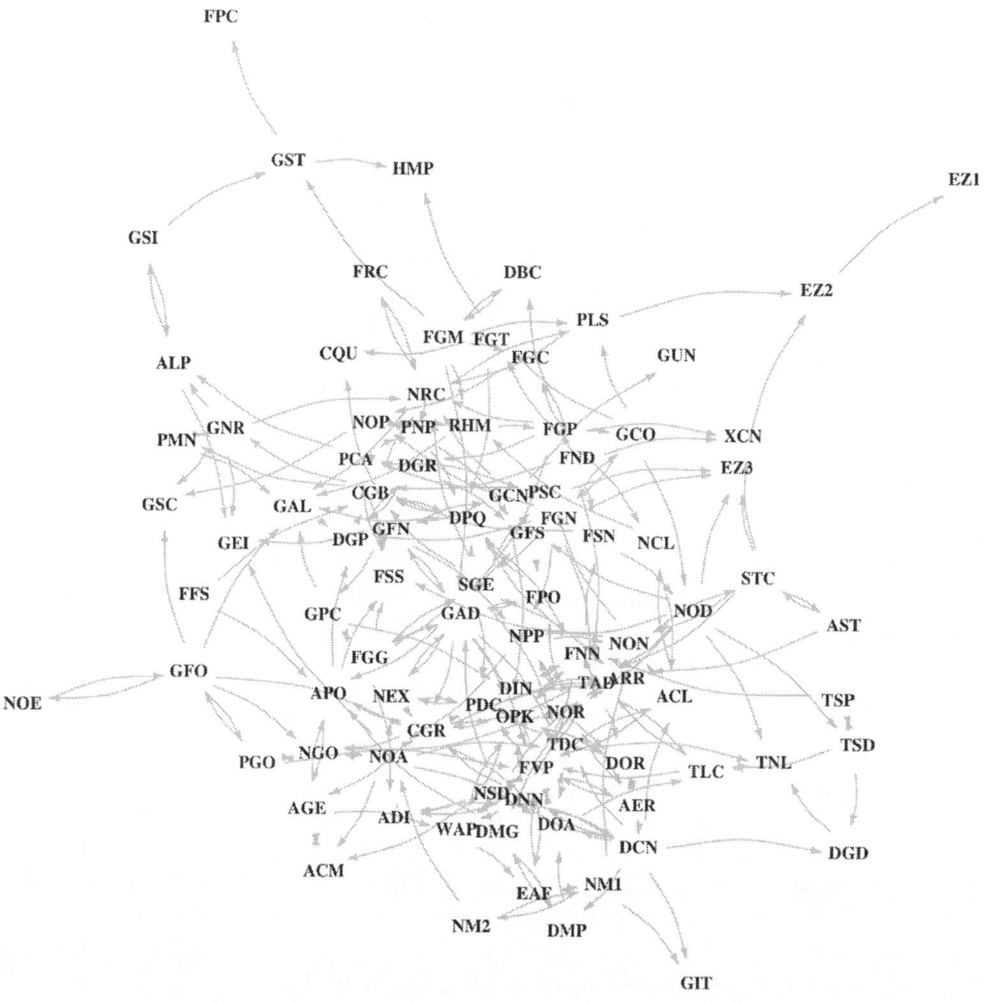

Figure 2: Full dependency graph

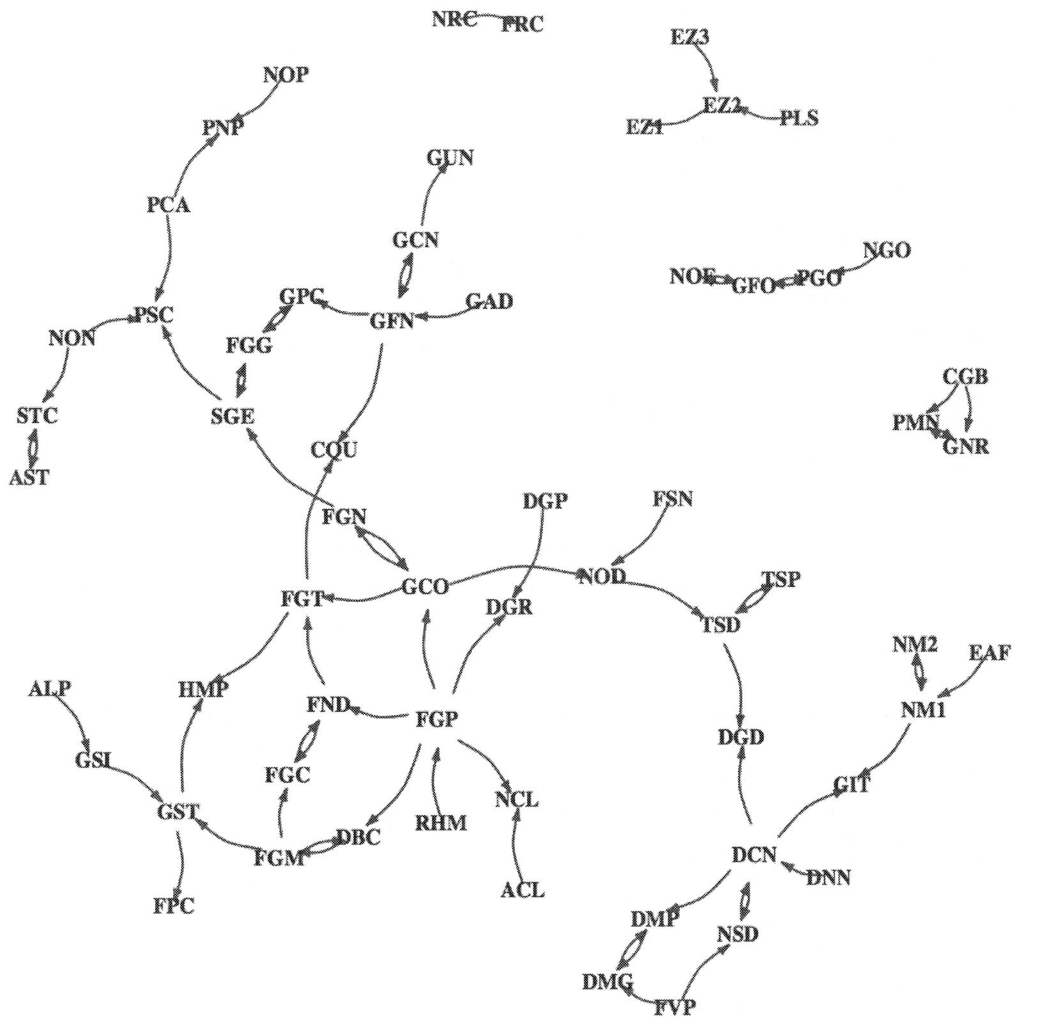

Figure 3: Partial dependency graph constructed from implications with up to two antecedents

4 Discussion

The results reported here show that applying machine learning techniques to the data can reveal previously unknown dependencies between parameters, leading to a potentially significant reduction in the search space of possible languages. The data contains more features than data points, which can make for the generation of spurious rules. The most obvious way to counteract this, adding more languages, comes at a very high cost, as it requires well-trained linguists. One can also use Occam's Razor and limit the search space of possible rules by limiting the number of antecedents in the rule, e.g. to two as we did here. Yet another approach is to collect data selectively for rules of interest, as only a small number of parameters, e.g. 2–3 per language, will be needed to test each rule.

This research could have important implications for the understanding of processes underlying the faculty of language (potentially strengthening the case for UG), with implications ranging from models of language acquisition to historical linguistics, where the syntactic relatedness between two languages may be more adequately measured. However, the approach requires a close collaboration between a machine learning expert, discovering empirical laws in the data, and a linguist who can test their plausibility and theoretical consequences. There is also an open theoretical computational learning challenge here presented by the need to estimate the significance of empirical findings from a given number of examples (languages) with respect to the available range of discriminative features in the dataset.

References

M. Baker. 2001. *The Atoms of Language*. Basic Books, New York.

L. Bortolussi, G. Longobardi, C. Guardiano, and A. Sgarro. 2011. How many possible languages are there? In G. Bel-Enguix, V. Dahl, and M.D. Jiménez-López, editors, *Biology, Computation and Liguistics*, IOS, Amsterdam, pages 168–179.

N. Chomsky. 1964. *Current issues in linguistic theory*. Mouton, The Hague.

N. Chomsky. 1981. *Lectures on Government and Binding*. Foris, Dordrecht.

R. Clark and I. Roberts. 1993. A computational model of language learnability and language change. *Linguistic Inquiry* 24:299–345.

C. Guardiano and G. Longobardi. 2005. Parametric comparison and language taxonomy. In M. Batllori, M. L. Hernanz, C. Picallo, and F. Roca, editors, *Grammaticalization and parametric variation*, OUP, Oxford, pages 149–174.

M. Hall, E. Frank, G. Holmes, B. Pfahringer, P. Reutemann, and I. H. Witten. 2009. The WEKA data mining software. *ACM SIGKDD Explor. Newsl.* 11:149–174.

D. W. Lightfoot. 2017. Discovering new variable properties without parameters. *Linguistic Analysis* 41. Special edition: Parameters: What are they? Where are they?

G. Longobardi. 2005. A minimalist program for parametric linguistics? In H. Broekhuis, N. Corver, M. Huybregts, U. Kleinhenz, and J. Koster, editors, *Organizing Grammar: Linguistic Studies*, Mouton de Gruyter, Berlin/New York, pages 407–414.

G. Longobardi and C. Guardiano. 2009. Evidence for syntax as a signal of historical relatedness. *Lingua* 119(11).

G. Longobardi, C. Guardiano, G. Silvestri, A. Boattini, and A. Ceolin. 2013. Toward a syntactic phylogeny of modern Indo-European languages. *Journal of Historical Linguistics* 3(1):122–152.

T. Mitchell. 1997. *Machine Learning*. MIT.

R. Quinlan. 1986. Induction of decision trees. *Machine Learning* 1(1):81–106.

R. Quinlan. 1993. *C4.5: Programs for Machine Learning*. Morgan Kaufmann Publ., San Matteo, CA.

I.G. Roberts. 2012. On the nature of syntactic parameters: a programme for research. In C. Galves, S. Cyrino, R. Lopes, F. Sandalo, and J. Avelar, editors, *Parameter Theory and Language Change*, Oxford University Press, Oxford, pages 319–334.

Appendix A: List of Parameters

FGP	gramm. person
FGM	gramm. Case
FPC	gramm. perception
FGT	gramm. temporality
FGN	gramm. number
GCO	gramm. collective number
PLS	plurality spreading
FND	number in D
NOD	NP over D
FSN	feature spread to N
FNN	number on N
SGE	semantic gender
FGG	gramm. gender
CGB	unbounded sg N
DGR	gramm. amount
DGP	gramm. text anaphora
CGR	strong amount
NSD	strong person
FVP	variable person
DGD	gramm. distality
DPQ	free null partitive Q
DCN	article-checking N
DNN	null-N-licensing art
DIN	D-controlled infl. on N
FGC	gramm. classifier
DBC	strong classifier
GSC	c-selection
NOE	N over ext. arg.
DMP	def matching pronominal possessives
DMG	def matching genitives
GCN	Poss°-checking N
GFN	Gen-feature spread to Poss°
GAL	Dependent Case in NP
GUN	uniform Gen
EZ1	generalized linker
EZ2	non-clausal linker
EZ3	non-genitive linker
GAD	adpositional Gen
GFO	GenO
PGO	partial GenO
GFS	GenS
GIT	Genitive-licensing iterator
GSI	grammaticalised inalienability
ALP	alienable possession
GST	grammaticalised Genitive
GEI	Genitive inversion
GNR	non-referential head marking
HMP	NP-heading modifier

AST	structured APs
STC	structured cardinals
GPC	gender polarity cardinals
PMN	personal marking on numerals
CQU	cardinal quantifiers
PCA	number spread through cardinal adjectives
FFS	feature spread to structured APs
ADI	D-controlled infl. on A
PSC	number spread from cardinal quantifiers
RHM	Head-marking on Rel
FRC	verbal relative clauses
NRC	nominalised relative clause
NOR	NP over verbal relative clauses/ adpositional genitives
AER	relative extrap.
ARR	free reduced rel
DOR	def on relatives
NOP	NP over non-genitive arguments
PNP	P over complement
NPP	N-raising with obl. pied-piping
NGO	N over GenO
NOA	N over As
NM2	N over M2 As
NM1	N over M1 As
EAF	fronted high As
NON	N over numerals
FPO	feature spread to genitive postpositions
ACM	class MOD
DOA	def on all +N
NEX	gramm. expletive article
NCL	clitic poss.
PDC	article-checking poss.
ACL	enclitic poss. on As
APO	adjectival poss.
WAP	wackernagel adjectival poss.
AGE	adjectival Gen
OPK	obligatory possessive with kinship nouns
TSP	split deictic demonstratives
TSD	split demonstratives
TAD	adjectival demonstratives
TDC	article-checking demonstratives
TLC	Loc-checking demonstratives
TNL	NP over Loc
XCN	conjugated nouns

Association for Computational Linguistics
209 N. Eighth Street
Stroudsburg, Pennsylvania 18360

ISBN 978-1-5108-5548-9

CURRAN ASSOCIATES INC.
proceedings.com

1st Workshop on Natural Language Generation, Evaluation and Metrics (GEM 2021)

Held online due to COVID-19

5-6 August 2021
Bangkok, Thailand